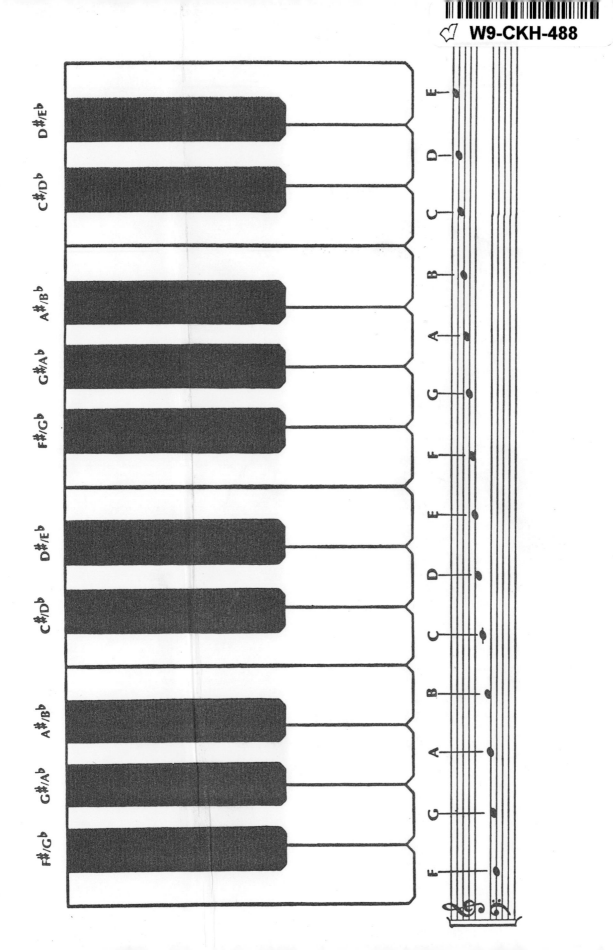

World of Music

Carmen E. Culp • Lawrence Eisman
Mary E. Hoffman
Authors

Carmino Ravosa • Phyllis Weikart
Theme Musical   **Movement**

Darrell Bledsoe
Producer, Vocal Recordings

Silver Burdett & Ginn

Morristown, NJ • Needham, MA

Atlanta, GA • Cincinnati, OH • Dallas, TX • Menlo Park, CA • Deerfield, IL

ISBN 0-382-07052-6

Contents

Music for Living   2

Introduction: New Beginnings   4

Chapter 1—A Blend of Two Worlds   8

A Trip to Another World (9) • Music of Two Worlds (10) • An American Song (11) • A Blend of These Two Worlds (12) • A Song of the Yoruba (12) • Your Own Rhythm Complex (13) • Different Words, but, Oh That Vocal Style! (14) • The Jazz Drummer (15) • From Whence Jazz? (16) • Call Chart 1 (17) • The Game Is Called by the Refferee (18) • Improvising, or "Making It Up" (18) • Syncopation (When You're Feeling Offbeat) (20) • A Piece That Africa Inspired (22) • Call Chart 2 (23)

Chapter 2—Style   24

Music in Stylish Clothing (26) • Making Comparisons (28) • Simplicity Then and Now (30) • Call Chart 3 (33) • How Different (34) • Even Symphonies Have Their Differences (36) • The Classic Period (38) • Painting in the Age of Reason (39) • How Do You Know If It's Classic? (40) • Adding Harmony (42) • All Together Now! (43) • Ludwig van Beethoven (46) • How Musicians Worked in Beethoven's Time (47) • A Servant Class (48) • Beethoven's Youth (49) • Beethoven, the Writer of Songs (50) • Beethoven the Idealist (50) • Egmont Overture (51) • Call Chart 4 (51) • The Romantic Period (52) • A Romantic Song (53) • The Twentieth Century—Our Contemporary Period (54) • The Twentieth Century Voice (56) • Modern Days, Modern Instruments (and a Few New Tricks) (58) • Melody (60) • Melody, Melody, Who Has the Melody? (62) • Rhythms Today (64) • Harmony—Wild and Wacky (66) • Tone Clusters (66) • Whatever You Do, Don't Pull the Plug! (68) • Call Chart 5 (69)

Chapter 3—Singing in Groups   70

Getting a Good Blend (70) • "Old Hundred" (72) • Monophonic and Polyphonic Textures (73) • Developing Breath Control (78) • Homophonic Texture (79) • Singing Partner Songs (80) • The Oratorio (82) • Singing as a Group (83) • Singing in Parts (84) • A German Folk Song (85) • Tests and What Do You Hear? Evaluations (86)

Understanding Music   92

Chapter 4—The Elements of Music   94

Melody (94) • Melody Steps Out (96) • Melody Leaps About (98) • And Finally (We Repeat), Notes Repeat (99) • All Steps Are Not Created Equal (100) • Step to the Piano, Maestro (101) • Scale Patterns—They Make a Difference (102) • Key Signatures (103) • The Minor Scale (104) • Call Chart 6 (105) • That Ol' Split-Level Scale (106) • And Now for a Brief Interval (108) • Melody—On It's Construction Site (110) • Sequence (111) • Variation and Contrast (112) • Add Rhythm to Move a Melody (113) • Clap a Rhythm, Call a Song! (114) • Beats in Groups (116) • Meter in 2 (116) • The Meter Signature (116) • Meter in 4 (116) • Meter in 3 (118) • Alternating 2 and 3 (A Neat Trick) (120) • The Long and the Short of It (122) • Music's Triple Threat—the Triplet (124) • And What Does That Little Dot Do? (125) • More on Syncopation (125) • Playing Along (126) • Tempo (128) • Harmony—Getting It All Together (130) • Harmony, Harmony, Quite Contrary (132) • Polyphonic Texture (133) • Tie the Music Up with Chords (135) • Tone Color—The Sounds of Music (136) • Sing Those Golden Tones (138) • Three Performers, One Piece (139) • Some Singers Do It All (139) • Instrumental Music's Four Basic Colors (140) • How's Your Color Sense? (141) • Call Chart 7 (141)

Chapter 5—Patterns into Form   142

Patterns in Sound (142) • Team Up with Your Pattern (144) • A Layer Cake of Patterns (145) • A Composer's Best Friend Is His Pattern (146) • Little Streams Make a River (146) • Patterns for Playing (148) • How's That Again? (149) • 3+2+2=7 (150) • More Beats Again—Meter in 10 (152) • Beats within Beats (or 6, 3, or 2?) (153) • Three as One (154) • Another Subdivision on the Musical Landscape (155) • An "Unsquare" Dance (156) • Diagramming Meter (158) • Bluesin' On the Bottom, Rockin' On the Top (160) • A Rock Progression We Have Known and Loved—I VI IV V_7 (161) • From Pattern to Piece (170) • Discern Those Devices! (That Means Recognize Them) (171) • Filling Out Forms (172) • Rondo—Music's Bad Penny (174) • A Rondo by Beethoven (174) • Call Chart 8 (175) • Tests and What Do You Hear? Evaluations (177)

Performing Music   182

Chapter 6—Performing in Ensembles   184

Building an Ensemble (185) • A Popular Trio (186) • Close Up the Ranks, Men! (187) • Two Parts—Duet and Chorus (188) • It's All in the Family (190) • The People's Choice (192) • An Unusual Instrument (193) • Sin ellos no hay fiesta (Without Them There's No Party!) (194) • The Sound of the Highlands (195) • And All That Jazz! (196) • A Classic Jazz Ensemble (198) • The Vocal Backups (199)

Chapter 7—Following a Score   200

The Full Score (202) • Pass the Theme, Please! (204) • You Can't Tell the Players Without a Score (206) • Call Chart 9 (207) • Careers in Music—Conducting (208)

Chapter 8—Don't Go Anywhere without a Song   210

A Theme Musical by Carmino Ravosa (210) • Don't Go Anywhere Without a Song (210) • I Like Me (213) • Everything's Coming Up Roses (214) • Never Say Never (215)

Chapter 9—Oliver!   216

The Story of Oliver Twist (216) • Act I, Scene I (216) • For Study (219) • Scene 2 (220) • For Study (220) • Scene 3 (224) • For Study (228) • For Study (229) • Act II, Scene 1 (233) • For Study (233) • Scene 2 (235) • Scene 3 (240) • Finale (245) • For Study (245) • Tests and What Do You Hear? Evaluations (246)

Sing and Celebrate   252

Reference Bank   306

Glossary   **306**
Can You Read This?   **308**
Sound Bank   **312**
Classified Index   **315**
Song Index   **317**
Picture Credits   **318**

MUSIC FOR LIVING

INTRODUCTION: BEGINNINGS

People make music in many ways. They play instruments with others in bands, orchestras, jazz ensembles, and rock groups. Or, they play by themselves on piano or organ, guitar or harmonica. Almost everyone can sing—from those who manage to belt out a tune in the shower to those who sing in folk groups, choirs, in opera houses, and in Broadway theaters. Some teach singing, or serve in churches and synagogues as choirmasters and cantors.

"Sing," on page 5, is all *about* singing. "Ja-Da," on page 6, is a song from the beginning of the jazz age. "Nine Hundred Miles," on page 7, is a lively song from the tradition of the black spiritual. Learn to sing these songs. Sing for the joy of it. Just relax, enjoy, and SING . . .

LISTENING SKILLS 1 *Collage of Musical Performers*

4

Sing

Words and Music by Joe Raposo

La la la la la, La la la la la la, La la la la la la la.___

(sing echo 2nd time)

Sing! Sing! Sing a song. Sing a song. Sing out loud. Sing out

loud. Sing out strong. Sing out strong. Sing of good things, not

bad. Sing of hap-py, not sad.

Sing! Sing! Sing a song. Sing a song. Make it

sim-ple to last your whole life long._____ Don't

wor-ry that it's not good e-nough, __ for an-y-one else to hear.

Sing! Sing a song!_____

(Repeat and fade)

La la la la la, La la la la la la, La la la la la la la.___

Ja-Da

Words and Music by Bob Carleton

1. You've heard all a - bout your rag - gy mel - o - dy, __ Ev - 'ry thing from op - 'ra down to
2. Our bands have been dig - ging back for tunes to be sung, __ Op - er - as and nurs - 'ry rhymes have

har - mo - ny, __ But I've a lit - tle song that I will sing to you, __ It's
been o - ver - done, __ I dug a lit - tle deep - er and I found this thing, __ It's

gon - na win you through and through. __ There's not much to the words but the
rag - time, but it still can swing. __ It's not a tur - key trot or a-

mu - sic is grand, __ And you'll be a - sing - ing it to beat __ the band. __ You've
shim - my one - step, __ But when grand - ma danced to it, she thought she was hep, __ It

heard of the tis - ket and tas - ket, it's true, __ But give a lit - tle lis - ten to this, __
still is a dit - ty, I'm sure you will find, __ Will keep a run - nin' 'round and a - round __

REFRAIN

__ will you? __ Ja - Da, _____ Ja - Da, _____
__ your mind. __

Ja - Da, Ja - Da, Jing, Jing, Jing, _____ Ja - Da, _____ Ja - Da, _____

Ja - Da, Ja - Da, Jing, Jing, Jing, ___ That's a fun - ny lit - tle bit of

mel - o - dy ___ It's so sooth - ing and ap - peal - ing to me, ___ It goes

Ja - Da, ___ Ja - Da, ___ Ja - Da, Ja - Da, Jing, Jing, Jing. ___

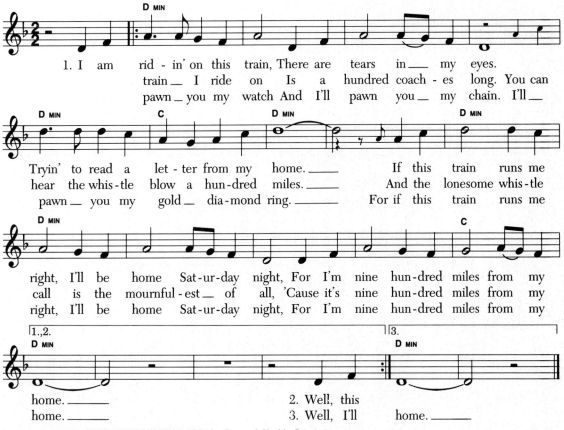

Nine Hundred Miles

Black American Work Song   Arranged and Adapted by Cisco Houston

1. I am rid - in' on this train, There are tears in ___ my eyes.
   train ___ I ride on Is a hundred coach - es long. You can
   pawn ___ you my watch And I'll pawn you ___ my chain. I'll ___

Tryin' to read a let - ter from my home. ___ If this train runs me
hear the whis - tle blow a hun - dred miles. ___ And the lonesome whis - tle
pawn ___ you my gold ___ dia - mond ring. ___ For if this train runs me

right, I'll be home Sat - ur - day night, For I'm nine hun - dred miles from my
call is the mournful - est ___ of all, 'Cause it's nine hun - dred miles from my
right, I'll be home Sat - ur - day night, For I'm nine hun - dred miles from my

[1., 2.]   [3.]

home. ___   2. Well, this
home. ___   3. Well, I'll   home. ___

The Slave Routes

British Colonies

Boston
New York
Philadelphia
Norfolk
Charles Town

New Orleans

Cuba
hispaniola
Porto Rico
Jamaica

Peru

Brazil

São Paulo

Bahia

São Paulo
Rio de Janiero

Africa

Saint Louis
Gorée

Cape Castle

São Paulo de Locanda

A Trip to Another World

Imagine! Your community is kidnapped by aliens from outer space. The people are taken to work as slaves in a galaxy far, far away!

Sound unbelievable? Something like that happened to thousands of people who lived in western and central Africa from the seventeenth through the nineteenth centuries. Rival groups sometimes captured their weaker neighbors and sold them to European and American sea captains. These sea captains took the captives to North and South America to be sold into slavery.

Some countries—Brazil, the Spanish and French islands in the Caribbean—allowed the slaves to retain their old-world customs, and so their music changed very little. Other countries, however, including the United States, would not allow slaves to practice their traditions. Even their music was forbidden. The slave owners in these countries were afraid that Africans would use their language and music to communicate secretly. The slave owners were right! Even though their language and music were forbidden, the Africans developed a musical style based on European traditions. This style allowed them to "talk" to one another, much as they had done in the lands that most would never see again. Some of the qualities that African music brought to the New World can be seen in the chart below.

QUALITIES OF AFRICAN MUSIC

1. **Importance of complex rhythm patterns**
2. **Importance of percussion instruments**
3. **Use of *polyrhythms* (two or more rhythms performed at the same time)**
4. **Rhythm patterns repeated over and over**

Music of Two Worlds

Think of African music. What do you hear? You probably hear rhythm—lots of rhythm! Of course, you may say that all music has rhythm. Ah, but African rhythm is unlike that of any other music. What creates that unique excitement and drive that African music has?

Many African groups develop a rhythm complex. Following the chart below and five nonpitched percussion instruments, you can perform a rough imitation of a rhythm complex. First recite the numbers in sequence to twelve over and over until you feel the beat securely. Then choose instruments and play only on the beat given in your rhythm line. For example, player A will play only on beats 1, 4, 7, and 10. Start slowly and eventually work up to a very fast rhythm. Try adding other instruments and making up new rhythm patterns.

RHYTHM COMPLEX

	1	2	3	4	5	6	7	8	9	10	11	12
A	1			4			7			10		
B		2	3		5	6		8	9		11	12
C	1		3		5	6		8		10	11	
D	1		3		5	6	7			10		
E	1		3			6		8	9			12

An English Song

Afro-American music evolved from the African slaves' overlay of American and European harmonic and melodic styles on African rhythmic and percussive practices. It may have sounded strong in the beginning! Learn to sing "Oh, Dear, What Can the Matter Be?", and then listen on page 12 to what can be done with it.

Oh, Dear! What Can the Matter Be?

English Folk Song

A Blend of These Two Worlds

Here is "Oh, Dear, What Can the Matter Be?" combined
with the rhythm complex. The rhythm complex is normally an
accompaniment for singing or dancing, so there is usually a melody
sung over it. Of course, it is doubtful that any African group ever
sang "Oh, Dear" to a rhythm complex. But it does seem likely that
American- and European-style melodies were sung to rhythm
complexes in this hemisphere.

 Oh, Dear! What Can the Matter Be? with rhythm complex

A Song of the Yoruba

In Nigeria the Yoruba (YAWR uh buh) group worships a household
god called Elegua. When the Yoruba crossed the ocean to Cuba they
brought their beliefs with them, so it was natural for a song to be
written about Elegua. Although the language was Spanish and the
harmonies western, it is rhythmically African. Learn to sing
"Elegua," on page 13. How might it sound over the rhythm complex?

Elegua

Words and Music by Eduardo Davidson   English Words by Samuele Maquí

E - le - gua,   E - le - gua, san - to bo - ni - to;*___
eh - leh - gwah   eh - leh - gwah sahn - toh boh - nee - toh

E - le - gua,   E - le - gua, san - to chi - qui - to.†___ E - le - gua, ca -
eh - leh - gwah   eh - leh - gwah sahn - toh chee - kee - toh   eh - leh - gwah kah -
E - le - gua, you

ba - llo ne - gro___ con ban - de - ra co - lo - rao.   E - le - gua, ca -
bah - yoh neh - groh   kawn bahn - deh - rah koh - loh - rau   eh - leh - gwah kah -
ride a black horse___ and car - ry a scar - let flag.   *E - le - gua, you*

ba - llo ne - gro___ con ban - de - ra co - lo - rao.
bah - yoh neh - groh   kawn bahn - deh - rah koh - loh - rau
ride a black horse___ and car - ry a scar - let flag.

*lovely saint   †little holy doll

Your Own Rhythm Complex

You can make up your own rhythm complex. Here are the beginnings of it. You might play it using a cowbell on line A and maracas on line B.

```
    1 2 3 4 5 6 7 8
A.  1   3   5   7
B.  1 2 3 4 5 6 7 8
C.
D.
E.
```

Now, place numbers at random in the blank spaces. Don't use too many! There need to be spaces between the sounds to make your rhythm complex really interesting. Work out your rhythm complex and use it to accompany *Gitano,* performed by the group Santana.

Gitano . . . . Peraza

13

Different Words, But, Oh, That Vocal Style!

In this recording you will hear two singers. One is a black folk singer from Mississippi. The other is a singer from Upper Volta, a country on the west coast of Africa. What do you hear that is different in these songs? What is alike? Listen to the way both singers ornament the melodies. They slide up and down on the pitches, sometimes not even singing the exact pitches at all!

 Black-American and West African Vocal Styles

Now listen to Aretha Franklin singing *Soulville.*
Can you hear anything in her vocal style that is like that of the two folk singers?

 Soulville...Turner, Levy, Glover, and Washington

The Jazz Drummer

You've heard the word *polyrhythm* before. African music is filled with it. Your rhythm complex was a good example of polyrhythms in action. In the style known as "hot jazz"—jazz that is loud, fast, and rhythmic—the drummer may be the most important member of the ensemble, for it is he who keeps those African-inspired polyrhythms going. Listen to this drummer as he unleashes his polyrhythms in a furious drum solo.

 Drum solo—jazz style

Change the beat somewhere and the drummer can provide a rock rhythm background. Can you hear how the rhythms change in the rock-style solo?

 Drum solo—rock style

And how about our Latin American rhythms? They, too, are African in origin. In many ways they are more openly African than our American jazz or rock rhythms are. That is because, unlike slaves in the United States, slaves in Latin America were allowed to retain their cultural traditions. Latin American slaves had no need to alter their music as much as slaves in North America did.

 Drum solo—samba

From Whence Jazz?

Cultural traditions are so deeply ingrained in all of us that we can't help carrying them with us wherever we go. Even within the United States, if we move from one part of the country to another, we may find some cultural differences and bewildering habits. Other people may find our habits bewildering as well.

Slowly, however, we begin to blend our cultural patterns with those of the surrounding cultures. The African slaves did the same thing. Their music—rhythmic, driving, exciting—mixed with the European-based harmonies of the New World and created new kinds of music: spirituals, jubilees, and the only purely American musical style, jazz. The make-it-up vocal style of the African singer transferred easily to the compose-as-you-go instrumental style of the jazz musician.

Call Chart 1

Listen to Benny Goodman's *Seven Come Eleven*. It certainly doesn't sound African, but the way the instruments improvise can only be a reflection of the improvisations of the African musician. The Call Chart will help you identify each instrument.

(LISTENING SKILLS 1) *Seven Come Eleven* . . . . Benny Goodman

1. Drum set
2. Bass
3. Saxophone and vibraphone play theme
4. Clarinet improvisation with vibraphone accompaniment
5. Saxophone and vibraphone play theme
6. Guitar improvisation with vibraphone
7. Guitar with resonating vibraphone accompaniment
8. Guitar with vibraphone
9. Vibraphone improvisation with light clarinet accompaniment
10. Vibraphone improvisation
11. Clarinet improvisation
12. Saxophone and vibraphone play theme, ending in coda

The Game Is Called by the Rifferee

Riff! A most important word in jazz. A riff is an *ostinato* (ah stee NAH toh), that pattern of melody or harmony or rhythm (or any combination of the three) that repeats over and over and over. *Seven Come Eleven* has several riffs. Here are some of the more noticeable ones. If you listen to the Call Chart on page 17 again, you will hear these riffs at the calls shown.

Improvising, or "Making It Up"

In the recording on page 14, you heard how African and Black-American musicians made up music with their voices. Making up music on the spot is called *improvising*. African musicians also improvise on percussion instruments. And, as you have learned, African vocal improvisation was picked up in this country by instrumental musicians. What a curious development—an African vocal style that became a North American instrumental style!

In jazz, everyone improvises, whether the musician plays a pitched or a nonpitched instrument. Jazz players improvise on a chord scheme. A chord is any three or more notes with different letter names sounded together. But in jazz the chords have to be very specific. You will need five chords to improvise on *Seven Come Eleven*. Line up bells so that they look like those on page 19.

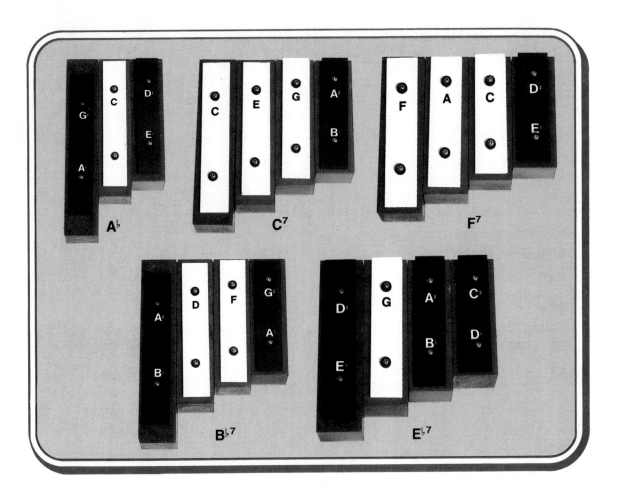

In this chart each box represents a measure. One student will be assigned to each chord. When your turn comes, improvise a rhythm on the chord during that measure. You can play two or three notes at once or just play up and down the bells.

Section

A	$A^\flat$	$A^\flat$	$A^\flat$	$A^\flat$	$A^\flat$	$A^\flat$	$A^\flat$	$A^\flat$
A	$A^\flat$	$A^\flat$	$A^\flat$	$A^\flat$	$A^\flat$	$A^\flat$	$A^\flat$	$A^\flat$
B	C^7	C^7	F^7	F^7	$B^{\flat 7}$	$B^{\flat 7}$	$E^{\flat 7}$	$E^{\flat 7}$
A	$A^\flat$	$A^\flat$	$A^\flat$	$A^\flat$	$A^\flat$	$A^\flat$	$A^\flat$	$A^\flat$

You can improvise with the musicians on *Seven Come Eleven,* using this chord pattern. Here is *Seven Come Eleven* without call numbers. Listen for the drum introduction and begin playing when the bass begins.

Seven Come Eleven (without call numbers).....Goodman

Syncopation
(When You're Feeling Offbeat)

Listen to this recording of "Comedy Tonight."
What do you notice about the rhythms of the
words and music?

A Funny Thing Happened on the
Way to the Forum,
"Comedy Tonight" .... Sondheim

There is a striking rhythm pattern that recurs again and again. It
can be written like this:

The pattern is *syncopated*. That is, strong emphasis is given to
something that should be weak. Let's write it another way.

Can you see that the middle eighth notes are tied together as one
note? That gives an emphasis to the weak part of the first beat and
makes it sound—well—jazzy! And while syncopation has been a
part of Western musical tradition for over 600 years, African music
certainly focused attention on it. Syncopation can change the
character of a piece of music entirely. On page 21 are two examples
of the same song, "You Are My Sunshine." Learn to sing it the way
it was originally written. Then listen to it performed in a jazzy,
syncopated version.

You Are My Sunshine

Words and Music by Jimmie Davis and Charles Mitchell

You are my sun - shine, _____ my on - ly sun - shine; _____

_ You make me hap - py _____ when skies are gray. _____

_ You'll ne - ver know, dear, _____ how much I love you; _____

_ Please don't take my sun - shine a - way. _____

Syncopated version

You are my sun - shine, _ my on - ly sun - shine; _ You make me

hap - py __ when skies are gray. You'll nev - er know, dear, _

how much I love you; _ Please don't take my _ sun - shine a - way. __

A Piece That Africa Inspired

The percussion section! Our melodic instruments, such as the clarinet, flute, trumpet, and all the strings, are European in origin, but our percussion instruments owe much to Africa. The xylophone (with its relatives the vibraphone and marimba), the tom-tom, the maracas, the claves, the slit drum, the conga drum, and many others, are all derived from African influences. How much less interesting our American music might be today had it not been for the enrichment by Africans.

Afro-Amero, a piece for percussion ensemble, was inspired by Phil Faini's (fah EE nee) studies in Africa. It was composed so that school students could perform African rhythms, using instruments that might be found in the school percussion ensemble. There is a main theme that looks like this. Play it on bells or on the piano.

All the other themes are rhythmic. The main rhythmic theme looks like this. Try playing it on a nonpitched percussion instrument.

Follow the Call Chart on page 23 to show you what happens in the piece.

Call Chart 2

Afro-Amero . . . . Faini

1. Main rhythmic theme; marimba; rhythm again

2. Melodic theme appears; slow tempo

3. Loud main rhythmic theme; *p*, followed by layering of rhythms

4. Timpani

5. Tom-tom leading to (>) sudden stop; short, sharp patterns and silences

6. Rhythmic theme and melodic theme at the same time; melody, in smaller note values, moves faster now; again sudden stop; short, sharp patterns and silences

7. Strong rhythm ♪♪ ♪ ♪♪ ♪♪ ♪♪ ; timpani begins layering rhythms

8. Melody, in still smaller note values, moves even faster; energetic rhythm of call No. 7 reappears *ff*

9. Layering of rhythms begins (polyrhythms), ——— *ff*

10. Melody in even smaller note values and slightly syncopated; ——— coda

CHAPTER 2—STYLE

"You're right in style."

"That's not my style."

"That suit is definitely out of style."

How often have you heard expressions like these? *Style* is something that affects us in many ways. Often we are unaware of the effect of style on our lives.

What *is* style? *Style* is the appearance of an object— a painting, a building, a suit of clothes, a pair of shoes, an automobile. Even as seemingly insignificant an item as a pencil has a style. Everything has style. If the style is a current one, we say it is "in style." If the style is old-fashioned, we say it is "out of style."

Ezra Stoller © ESTO

Music, too, has styles. They usually last longer than clothing or automobile styles. They last so long that we usually group them into large time periods and give them names. For example, the Classic period includes music that was written in Classic style. And the Modern period includes music in Modern style.

Here are two short excerpts from compositions that are rather long. The first is by Mozart, considered by many to be one of the greatest composers of all time. The second excerpt is by Schoenberg (SHUHRN behrg), a composer of our own twentieth century—the modern period.

 Concerto No. 21 in C Major for Piano and Orchestra, Movement 2 (excerpt)..........................Mozart

 Concerto for Piano and Orchestra, Movement 1 (excerpt) ....Schoenberg

Each piece has an obvious melody. Follow the melodies as you listen to them again.

Mozart

Schoenberg

And each piece has some simple accompanying harmony.

Mozart   **Schoenberg**

Schoenberg, *Piano Concerto* © MCMXLIV by G. Schirmer, Inc. International Copyright Secured. Printed in the U.S.A.

The pieces sound very different in their melodies and harmonies, even though there are some similarities. Both concertos are written for a piano soloist with an orchestra of strings, winds, and percussion. What is different about these pieces is their *style*. One, by Mozart, is written in Classic style—a style that prevailed from about 1750 to about 1815. The other, by Schoenberg, is in a more dissonant twentieth-century style, a *modern* style.

Music in Stylish Clothing

The clothing in these two pictures is from the twentieth century. What is it about the clothes that makes you know they are from the same time period? There is something about the materials, the cut, and the casual look of the clothing that tells you, "This is mine. This is from my time." Sometimes it's hard to describe exactly how we recognize a style from our time period. Perhaps books, magazines, movies, and television have made us familiar with the clothing of other eras so that we can compare them with our own clothing. For instance, the men in the pictures on page 27 are both wearing suits, but one suit is obviously from the twentieth century, and the other is from the Classic period.

It seems pretty obvious that recognizing clothing styles is largely a matter of making comparisons. Recognizing musical styles is no different. We can compare and contrast two pieces of music, finding out the likenesses and the differences. Then we can make a judgment about these styles.

What exactly do we compare? We have to look at the specifics of our pieces—melody, harmony, rhythm, words (if the pieces are vocal works), tone color, and any other clue we might detect to help us see likenesses and differences.

Making Comparisons

Here is a song you can sing. Listen to the recording and follow the words and music. Then try singing along with the recording or with the piano accompaniment that your teacher or another student might play.

Where Have All the Flowers Gone?

Words and Music by Pete Seeger

1. Where have all ___ the flow - ers gone, ___ Long time ___ pass - ing, ___
2. Where have all ___ the young girls gone, ___ Long time ___ pass - ing, ___

Where have all ___ the flow - ers gone, ___ Long time a - go,
Where have all ___ the young girls gone, ___ Long time a - go,

Where have all ___ the flow - ers gone, ___ Young girls ___ picked them ev-'ry one. ___
Where have all ___ the young girls gone, ___ Gone to young men ev-'ry one, ___

When will they ev - er learn, _____ when will they ev - er learn?
When will they ev - er learn, _____ when will they ev - er learn?

3. Where have all the young men gone, long time passing. . .
Where have all the young men gone, they are all in uniform. . .

4. Where have all the soldiers gone, long time passing. . .
Where have all the soldiers gone, gone to graveyards ev'ry one. . .

5. Where have all the graveyards gone, long time passing. . .
Where have all the graveyards gone, covered with flowers ev'ry one. . .

6. Where have all the flowers gone. . .

Now listen to the next piece. It is a piece by Haydn, a Classic-period composer. What kind of comparison can you make between this piece and "Where Have All the Flowers Gone"?

St. Anthony Chorale . . . . Haydn

You've sung the song and listened to the *St. Anthony Chorale*. Let's look at a chart to see the likenesses and the differences in the two pieces.

	"Where Have All the Flowers Gone?"	*St. Anthony Chorale*
Tone Color	Voice and Piano	Organ
Melody	Clear, strong melody	Clear, strong melody
Rhythm	Relaxed; sometimes on the beat, sometimes syncopated	On the beat, like a hymn or patriotic song
Harmony	Harmony is an accompaniment to the singer.	Mostly three or four basic chords
Form	Simple phrase repetition with slight variations on phrase endings	ABA

Wes Montgomery, a guitarist, has put the two pieces together. The *Chorale* is always played by trumpets; the guitar plays "Where Have All the Flowers Gone?". Listen to the way Montgomery blends the eighteenth and twentieth centuries.

Where Have All the Flowers Gone? . . . . Seeger

29

Simplicity Then and Now

Westward ho! Manifest Destiny! Go West, young man! These are all phrases that led thousands and thousands of men and women in America to move westward in the nineteenth century. The people traveled on horseback and in covered wagons. Many simply *walked* across the prairies and mountains to find homes in the western territories of the young United States. The Indians, native peoples who had dwelled on the continent for centuries, resisted with fury the encroachment on their land. This dramatic period in the history of the United States is reflected in countless folk songs and ballads. The music has a similarity of harmony, easy-to-sing melodies, and simple rhythms that fall mainly on the beat, like the three cowboy songs in the medley, "Songs of the West."

Songs of the West

Arranged by Linda Williams

Red River Valley

1. From this val - ley they say you are go - ing, _____ We will
sit by my side if you love me, _____ Do not

2nd Time Only

sit by my side if you love me, _____ Do not

miss your bright eyes and sweet smile; _____ For they say you are tak - ing the
has - ten to bid me a - dieu; _____ But re - mem - ber the Red Riv - er

has - ten to bid _ me a - dieu, a - dieu; But the Red Riv - er

sun - shine _____ that bright - ens our path - way a - while. 2. Come and
val - ley _____ And the

Val - ley And the 2. Come and

girl. . . . 1. As I _ walked out in the streets of La - re - do, As
you are a cow - boy," These

girl who has loved you so true. Slow - ly,

(2nd Time Only)

I walked out in La - re - do one day, I spied a young cow - boy wrapped
words he said as I bold - ly walked by. "Come lis - ten to me and I'll

play the fife low - ly. He was a young

up   in white li - nen, wrapped up   in white li - nen and   cold   as   the clay. 2. "I
tell   my sad sto - ry.   I'm   shot   in   the   chest and   I'm

cow   -   boy,   but   he   had   done wrong and he's

see   by your out - fit   that   sure   I   will   die   to - day." _____

SOLO   *I Ride an Old Paint*

2. Bang   the drum   dy   -   ing.   I   ride   an old paint, and   I

He done   wrong,   he done

lead   an old dan, I'm   goin' to Mon - tan' for   to   throw the hou - li - han.   They

wrong,   A young cow   -   boy, _____   He done

feed   in the cou - lees,   they   wa - ter in the draw,   Their   tails   are all   mat - ted and their

wrong. _____   Ride a - round,   lit - tle do - gies, Ride a - round   them slow,   For the

ALL

backs   are all   raw.   Ride a - round,   lit - tle do - gies, Ride a - round   them slow,   For the

32

fier - y and snuff - y are rar - in' to go.

fier - y and snuff - y are rar - in' to go. For the fier - y and snuf - fy are

From this val - ley they say you are go - ing.

SOLO rar - in' to go. From this val - ley you are go - ing.

Call Chart 3

Here is a Call Chart on a piece from the Classic period. Listen to the composition as you follow it. How does this music compare to the songs in "Songs of the West"? Like the cowboy songs, it has a similarity of harmony, simple (that's the word!) melodies, and simple rhythms that fall mainly on the beat.

LISTENING SKILLS 2

Sonata No. 15 in C Major, K. 545, Movement 1
(excerpt) . . . . Mozart

1 First theme outlines chords

2 Scale passages upward and downward
3 Second theme

4 Chord passages—chords outlined
5 Closing passage, getting ready for the end

How Different Is Different?

Make a chart to show the similarities and differences between "Chester" and "NonChester." You can copy the chart below on a separate sheet of paper.

	"Chester"	"NonChester"
Rhythm, Beat		
Meter		
Form		
Note Value		
Melody Steps		
Leaps		
Singing Voice		
Speaking Voice		
Unusual Vocal Sounds		

Chester ②

Words and Music by William Billings

1. Let ty - rants shake their i - ron rod,
2. What grate - ful off' - ring shall _____ we bring,

And slav - 'ry clank _____ her gall - ing chains;
What shall we ren - der to _____ the Lord?

We fear them not, We _____ trust _____ in God;
Loud hal - le - lu - jahs _____ let _____ us sing,

New _____ Eng - land's God _____ for - ev - er reigns.
And _____ praise His name _____ on ev - 'ry chord.

34

NonChester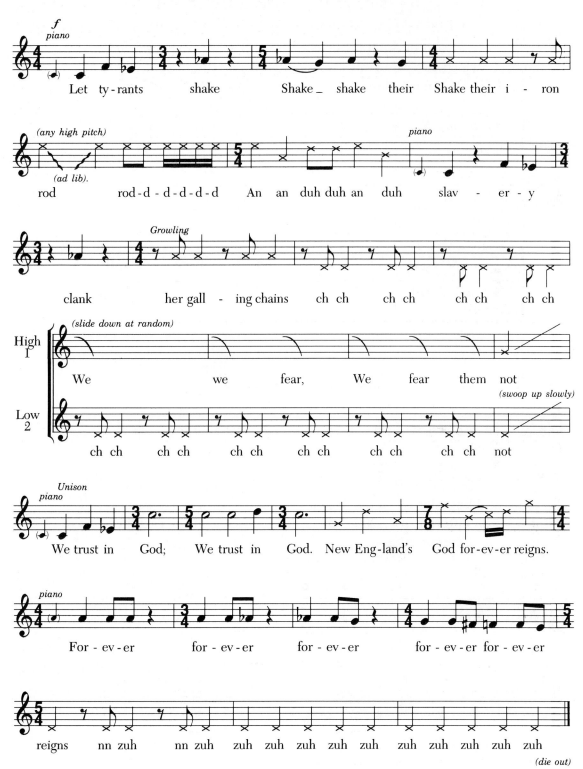

Words by William Billings   Music by Mary E. Hoffman

Even Symphonies Have Their Differences

"Chester" and "NonChester" have one thing in common—the words. Otherwise, one is hymnlike and solemn; the other is filled with different vocal sounds and erratic rhythms. Listen to these next two pieces. They, also, are in different styles. After you have listened to them, decide which list below most closely describes the Mozart piece and which list most closely describes the Shostakovich piece.

 Symphony No. 40 in G Minor, Movement 3 . . . . Mozart

 Symphony No. 1 in F, Movement 2 . . . . Shostakovich

	List 1	List 2
TONE COLOR	Full orchestra	Full orchestra, some piano
HARMONY	Little dissonance	Some dissonance
METER	Meter in 3	Meter in 2
MELODY	Singable	Not very singable
TEMPO	Tempo remains the same throughout	Tempo changes from fast to slow to fast

Mozart lived and composed during the Classic period—the latter half of the eighteenth century and the early nineteenth century. Shostakovich was a twentieth-century composer. He is a *contemporary* composer. Both men used the same musical materials, the same building blocks—pitch, rhythm, meter, tone color, and so forth. But the different ways they put these building blocks together created their different styles.

time TIME   *color* COLOR   *meter* METER

pitch PITCH   *rhythm* RHYTHM

Wolfgang Amadeus
Mozart
(1756–1791)

Mozart began his musical studies at an early age with his father, Leopold. Under Leopold's guidance young Wolfgang and his older sister, Nannerl, toured Europe as performers. One story told of Wolfgang (although probably just a legend) says he appeared before the royal family in Vienna. So taken was he with the young princess Marie Antoinette (who, as Queen of France, would lose her head during the French Revolution) that he leaped into her lap vowing to marry her when he grew up! Only a story, perhaps, yet it suggests the impact the gifted child must have had.

Mozart wrote in all the forms of the Classic period, enriching the world for centuries to come and representing the Classic period at its finest. His early death and his burial in an unmarked pauper's grave have not dimmed his brilliance.

Dimitri Shostakovich
(1906–1975)

Many feel that Shostakovich, a Soviet composer, is perhaps the finest symphony composer of the mid-twentieth century. His fifteen symphonies show not only a great deal of depth, but a struggle to be fresh and original without overstepping the bounds laid down by the government for a Soviet composer. The Soviet government insists that composers write within the style of "socialist realism"—a style that demands folk or folk-like elements, little dissonance, straightforward rhythms, simple harmonies, a patriotic element, and so forth.

In the beginning of his career, Shostakovich had composed in the dissonant style of the West, but the powerful Union of Soviet Composers, which policed such things, forced him to conform to the dictates of socialist realism. That Shostakovich was able to write such original works as his *Fifth Symphony* or the "Baba Yar" *Symphony* within the constrictions of socialist realism is a tribute to his genius.

The Classic Period

If you were asked to describe the building in this picture, what would you say about it? For one thing, it is beautifully proportioned. The columns are precisely placed to provide strength yet give a feeling of lightness, balance, and equality. The lines are clean and the decorations subtle. The building, a very ancient building found in Athens and called the Parthenon, is one of the world's greatest examples of Greek classic architecture.

About the middle of the eighteenth century, people became interested in the classicism of ancient Greek art and architecture. Greek philosophy was studied for its "modern" applications. Many people were curious to find answers to all sorts of questions in philosophy, art, religion, music, science, and technology. This time has been called the Age of Enlightenment, or the Age of Reason. The attempt to resurrect the ancient Greek culture resulted in the new Classic period.

Painting in the Age of Reason

David's *The Oath of the Horatii* is considered by many to be among
the finest examples of Classic paintings. The viewer can see at once
that the number *three* is of great importance to the artist. There are
three women at the right of the painting, and three young men are
taking an oath. The angle of the swords forms a triangle. The legs of
the men form other triangles, and there are three archways in the
rest of the room. The positions of the people in the painting create a
sense of balance. While two of the women are facing to the right—
out of the frame—the third is leaning in to the left, her head on the
shoulder of her kinswoman, her body and head angled back toward
the men. This creates a focus toward the center of the painting. The
two children—just by the contrast of being only two—point up the
pervading number three. Proportion and balance are key elements
in the Classic style.

The Oath of the Horatii
Jacques-Louis David

How Do You Know If It's Classic?

When you listen to a song on the radio, you can usually tell whether it's a rock song, a piece of jazz music, a Broadway show song, or a folk song. Sometimes you can even tell if the song was written in the 1920s or 1930s, the 1950s or 1970s, even the 1980s. That's because each type of song has its own style—those characteristics that set it apart in sound.

The music of the Classic period also has its own sound and style. Let's try putting a Classic piece together bit by bit. Here is a short melodic fragment. Sing it or play it.

Ex. 1

It doesn't sound finished, does it? It's too short. It needs something to balance it. Remember that Classic music is known for its sense of balance, of symmetry. So sing or play each of the following fragments. Which one seems to balance the first fragment best?

Ex. 2

Ex. 3

Ex. 4

Examples 2 and 4 don't seem to work. The shape of the melody is all wrong, and the notes don't seem to wind up in the right place. Example 3, on the other hand, is a good balance to Example 1. The melodic shape is exactly the same as in Example 1 but placed one pitch lower. Now it looks like this.

Ex. 5

You, your teacher, or another student can play the example on the piano or on bells.

A rhythm pattern adds interest to the melody.

Ex. 6

Our rhythm pattern continues, even though a new phrase is introduced. The composer has balanced the second phrase in a different way. The melody goes up until the middle of the phrase; then it goes down, still using the rhythm pattern. The rhythm pattern becomes a unifier, an element that holds everything together.

Phrase 1

Phrase 2

Adding Harmony

Our song is in the key of B♭. That means that notes in it are based on the B♭-major scale. On the staff, the B♭ major scale looks like this.

B♭ C D E♭ F G A B♭

Line up your bells on the B♭ scale and play it up and down to hear its "sound." Now set up those groups of bells like this.

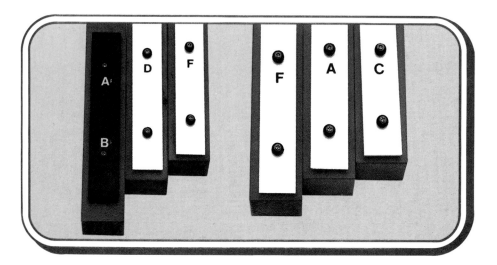

These chords are called *triads*. You can use them to add harmony to any Classic song. Try practicing the chords. Play this chord progression, using the B♭ and F triads.

B♭   B♭   F   F

Try singing along on the syllable *la*, using the first half of the phrase in Example 6 on page 41. Just as the melody seemed to need something to balance or complete it, the harmony seems unfinished as well. Try this progression on the second half of Example 6 on page 41. You will probably find it much more satisfying.

F   F   B♭   B♭

All Together Now!

Now play the chords while your classmates sing.

To harmonize a second part of the song, you will want a new chord—the C-major triad. On the staff it looks like this.

Line up your bells to look like this.

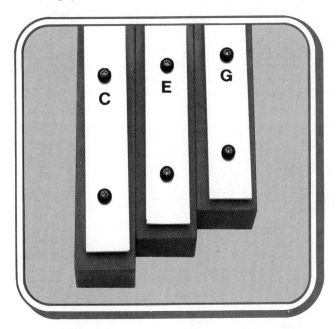

You need the C-major chord because the composition changes to a new key, from B♭ to F. Changing key is one of the most characteristic elements of Classic style. You will hear it again and again in the Classic works of many composers.

We have been constructing a song by Wolfgang Amadeus Mozart. It is the aria "In the Army," from *The Marriage of Figaro*. Play the chords as your classmates sing. Watch the *D.S. al Fine.* That means to go back to the sign 𝄋 and sing to the word *Fine*.

The Marriage of Figaro is an opera, a play set to music. Opera audiences applaud after a soloist finishes an aria like "In the Army" as well as after major duets, choruses, or other ensembles.

In the Army

from *The Marriage of Figaro*

Music by Wolfgang Amadeus Mozart

Ludwig van Beethoven

Events during Beethoven's Lifetime

1770—Beethoven is born.

1775—The American Revolution begins.

1776—The Declaration of Independence is ratified in Philadelphia.

1789—The French Revolution begins.

1791—The Bill of Rights becomes part of the Constitution of the
    United States of America.

1797—Franz Schubert is born.

1803—The Louisiana Purchase doubles the size of the United States.

1804—Nathaniel Hawthorne, America's first great novelist, is born.

1807—Beethoven's *Symphony No. 5 in C Minor* is completed.

1810—Beethoven's *Egmont Overture* is completed.

1812—The War of 1812, between the United States and Great
    Britain, begins.

1827—Beethoven dies in Vienna, Austria.

How Musicians Worked in Beethoven's Time

Musicians today have many outlets for their profession. Rock bands, church and synagogue choirs, orchestras, theaters, dance bands, and recording studios all provide opportunities for the working musician to earn a living. A few composers support themselves and their families by writing for Broadway, for films, for television, for opera houses, and for orchestras. Even fewer edit books on musical subjects, such as textbooks like this one. Many musicians teach privately. Others teach in public and private schools, in colleges, conservatories, and universities. Your own music teacher is one of these teaching musicians.

A Servant Class

In Beethoven's time, musicians were of the servant class. They usually served as church musicians or as "house" composers and conductors in the palace homes of the aristocracy. It was a secure job, usually meaning a small but steady income for life. Beethoven's father and grandfather had served the elector Franz Joseph, and everyone expected that young Ludwig, learning the viola and harpsichord with his father as his teacher, would follow his elders into the elector's service. From that beginning he would become the composer who, in many opinions, was one of the three or four greatest composers in history.

Beethoven's Youth

When we read about the growing-up years of famous composers, their childhoods so often seem to have been unhappy ones. Beethoven's early years were no exception. His alcoholic and overbearing father made a habit of waking the young Ludwig in the middle of the night, making him practice on the violin, viola, and at the pianoforte (as the early pianos were called) until sunrise. The exhausted boy was even discouraged from writing his own music. Instead the elder Beethoven insisted that his talented son practice only in preparation for his music lesson.

In spite of his father, young Beethoven managed to develop his considerable talent. He became an assistant organist and a violinist in the local court chapel and orchestra, positions that helped him to learn about the major composers of his time and about the instruments of the orchestra.

Beethoven, the Writer of Songs

Beethoven was not famed as a writer of songs, but this small round is typical of his sound and style.

The Metronome

Music by Ludwig van Beethoven   English Words by Georg von Sudland

Tick, tock, tick, tock, tick, tock, tick, tick-a tock, tick-a tock, tick-a tock, The met-ro-nome is_count-ing. Tick, tock, tick, tock, tick, tock, tick, tick, tock, Hear it count the time. Tick, tock, tick, tock, tick, tock, tick, tick, tock, Count-ing the tem-po and the time that it takes to per-form. Tick, tock, tick, tock, tick, tock, The might-y met-ro-nome is march-ing, march-ing, march-ing on.

Beethoven the Idealist

Beethoven's fame as a pianist spread quickly, and his reputation as a composer would soon grow to that of greatness. At the same time the ideals of the French Revolution of 1789—liberty, equality, and the fellowship of humankind—began to alter philosophical, social, and political thinking all over Europe. Beethoven, now a young man, found these principals of personal freedom deeply affecting. They would influence his choice of musical subjects until the end of his life, in such works as the *Symphony No. 9,* with its "Ode to Joy"; the opera *Fidelio;* and the *Egmont Overture.*

Egmont Overture

Beethoven's love of freedom drew him to a play by Goethe (GUHR tuh), the great German poet and playwright. The play's background is the revolt of the Dutch against their Spanish oppressors during the sixteenth century.

To support his growing empire, King Philip of Spain seized the Netherlands. The Dutch revolt in 1566 brought in the Spanish duke of Alba to crush the rebellion. The duke had thousands of people tortured and killed.

Now appeared the Duke of Egmont, a Dutch nobleman whose defiance of Alba led him to the gallows. In Goethe's play, Egmont's wife, Clarchen (CLAHR khehn), visits him in a dream as he lies in his cell waiting for execution.

"Your death will inspire the Dutch to rise up against the Spanish and overthrow them," she tells the awestruck Egmont. And at the gallows the next morning, he calls upon the Dutch to take pride in their heritage and win freedom for themselves once again.

Call Chart 4

Listen to a Call Chart on the Overture to *Egmont*. The number will help you discover what is happening in the music.

 Egmont Overture . . . . Beethoven

1.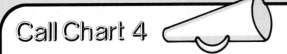
2. As at beginning   3. (strings, flute) 4. Egmont's theme
5. (strings, flute, bassoon) <
6. New theme
7. Egmont's theme
8. Same as 5
9. ▌▌▌▌ *f*
10. (timpani, strings, trumpet) *ff*
11. Full orchestra *ff*

51

The Romantic Period

"I'm an individual, and I'm going to do my own thing."

"I need to express myself in my own way and for myself alone."

"When I compose, I want to use more instruments and write for the largest orchestra ever!"

"The piano is my instrument of choice. I'll write piano music of technical brilliance!"

These are not the sentiments of young twentieth-century composers. These were the sentiments of composers who lived in the nineteenth century, a period we know as the Romantic period. The composers in the Romantic period were interested in expanding the whole musical vocabulary. Harmony became thick with notes, and dissonance began to play a more expressive part. Long melodies were written to provoke a strong emotional response. Form was expanded to become a loose framework on which to hang the beautiful melodies and harmonies. Listen to a piano piece by Liszt. Can you hear these characteristics in this work?

Concert Etude No. 3 in D♭ Major ("Un Sospiro") .... Liszt

Franz Liszt
(1811–1886)

Franz Liszt was the first solo concert performer. His piano virtuosity reshaped forever the way composers would think about this truly Romantic instrument. In the *Etude* "Un Sospiro" by Liszt you heard a broad melody sustained by an accompaniment of notes that seemed to cascade from the instrument. And you heard harmonies that were intended to make the listener feel deeply about the music. Liszt, along with Schubert, Schumann, and Chopin, was a typical example of the Romantic composer. He was a flamboyant figure who led a life that we associate today with movie stars or rock stars. Yet, he had a religious need (also typically Romantic) that led him to take minor orders in the Roman Catholic Church. To the end of his life he was called "Abbé Liszt" ("Father Liszt").

A Romantic Song

Johannes Brahms was a friend of Liszt and was a famous nineteenth-century composer himself. He wrote many pieces for all kinds of instrumental combinations. Many people like his songs best, especially his settings of folk songs. Romantic-period composers were fond of folk music and tried to incorporate it into their music.

Learn to sing "How Troubled the Waters." How is it different from the Classic pieces you have heard?

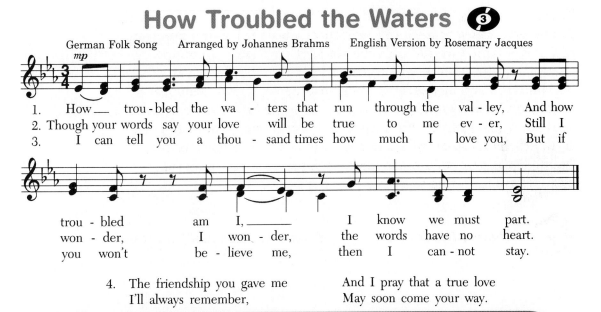

How Troubled the Waters

German Folk Song   Arranged by Johannes Brahms   English Version by Rosemary Jacques

1. How— trou-bled the wa - ters that run through the val - ley, And how
2. Though your words say your love will be true to me ev - er, Still I
3. I can tell you a thou - sand times how much I love you, But if

trou - bled   am   I, _____   I   know   we   must   part.
won - der,   I   won - der,   the   words   have   no   heart.
you   won't   be - lieve   me,   then   I   can - not   stay.

4. The friendship you gave me
   I'll always remember,

And I pray that a true love
May soon come your way.

Johannes Brahms
(1833–1897)

Johannes Brahms wrote far more than songs. His four symphonies are considered among the best of the Romantic period. While still a young man, Brahms had the good fortune to be befriended by the German composer Robert Schumann, with whom he lived and studied. This friendship (along with that of Robert's wife, Clara, who was a fine composer and concert pianist herself) tied Brahms to one of the first great composers of the Romantic movement in music. He had the misfortune to be placed by the media, as well as by his supporters, in a rivalry with Richard Wagner. It was a rivalry neither Brahms nor Wagner felt, and each had only good words for the other. At the end of his life Brahms became a familiar sight in the streets of Vienna, his portly figure supporting a beard and large hat.

The Twentieth Century—Our Contemporary Period

At the time a piece of music is written, it is always "contemporary." *Contemporary* is a big word meaning "with the times." We are living in the latter part of the twentieth century. This is *our* contemporary period. The twentieth century has seen many style changes in printing, music, architecture, and clothing, just to name a few areas. Look at the baseball uniforms above. The one on the left is from the beginning of our century. The one on the right is from more recent years. You see they are both baseball uniforms, because the basic form is the same. But they are different in certain details. The caps are different, as are the sleeves and trousers. Yet they are both products of the twentieth century—our own century. How do you think baseball uniforms will look a century from now?

If the twentieth century could be called anything at all (as the eighteenth century was called the Age of Reason), it might be called the Age of Technology. Everything in our society has been touched by the technological achievements of our century. The upper stamp below commemorates Wilbur and Orville Wright's first "flying machine" (the term *airplane* did not appear until several years later). This grand technological achievement of 1903 led directly to the event commemorated in the bottom stamp below, the landing of a man on the moon on July 20, 1969.

Think of other technological developments of our century—the supersonic jet plane, the telephone, the automobile, the X ray, television, computers. Can you imagine someone from the eighteenth century suddenly waking up today! Sounds like an idea for a TV sitcom. Changes are happening so fast we can hardly keep track of them. Can you name any performing group that was on the Top 40 charts five years ago? Three years ago? Last year? Last month? Things are happening fast in music, too.

The Twentieth-Century Voice

Our century has been marked by countless experiments in finding
new sounds. Sometimes the sounds have come from standard
instruments. Jazz singers have developed a technique called *scat
singing*. They use no words, only syllables, and the effect is like that
of an instrumental solo. Listen to Ella Fitzgerald as she sings *Some
of These Days* using scat syllables.

 Some of These Days . . . . Brooks-Vogel

Sometimes composers have experimented with the human voice,
asking it to do things not heard of until this century. Arnold
Schoenberg, a composer in the first half of the twentieth century,
asks the singer to create all sorts of new vocal effects in his song
cycle *Pierrot lunaire* ("The Clown Pierrot by Moonlight"). Listen to
"The Dandy" from this song cycle. In it Pierrot describes how he
uses moonlight to paint his face so that he can look like a dandy—
someone who is always well dressed, if a little overly so, and ready
for a party. The vocal technique is called *Sprechstimme* (SHPREHKH
shtih muh, or speech-voice), something that is part song, part speech.

 Pierrot lunaire, "The Dandy" . . . . Schoenberg

This composition for voice and piano calls for four kinds of vocal sounds: groans, hisses, lip pops, and sighs. Also, there is one pitch to be played on the piano (or any other instrument): C♯. You and your classmates can split into four sections and work out the piece. There is no meter, so watch the clock to time the sections. If a box is empty, do nothing. If a line thickens, make the sound louder. If a line is wavy, make the sound with a wide vibrato. If a line or dot is high in the box, make a high sound. If it is low in the box, make a low sound. This kind of notation has been called in the twentieth century *graphic notation*. Have fun with it!

See Sharp   Mary E. Hoffman

	5 Sec.	10 Sec.	5 Sec.	5 Sec.	10 Sec.	1 Sec.
Groan	————		▬ ▬ ▬ ▬		∿∿∿	▬
Hiss	– – – – ————		▬▬▬		– – – – – – · ·	▬
Lip Pop		• • • • • • •		• • • · ·		●
Sigh		∿∿∿∿	∿∿∿	↘	▬
Piano		(notation)	(notation)		(notation)	(notation)

Making Graphic Notation Your Own

You can create your own piece using graphic notation. With your classmates make up a vocal or instrumental sound for each symbol in the box at the right. Put the symbols on the board in a specific order, then perform the piece. Try creating a piece for three or four independent voices or instruments.

Modern Days, Modern Instruments (and a Few New Tricks)

Did you ever think a radio could be a musical instrument? Well, John Cage did. This highly original American composer wrote a piece for twelve radios called *Imaginary Landscape,* No. 4. Players tune to any station and turn the volume up or down as the conductor dictates. And how about the tape recorder? Almost from the beginning of tape-recording techniques, composers have experimented with creating new sounds using the tape recorder. Listen to this recording of a tape "classic" by Canadian composer Hugh LeCaine. LeCaine used a single drop of water to create all the effects.

3 LISTENING SKILLS   *Dripsody* .... LeCaine

How could so many different sounds be created by a tape recorder? Some ways were to record at one speed and play back at another, making the sound higher or lower, and to edit the tape so that the sounds were faster or slower, shorter or longer. Sometimes, LeCaine put two versions of the drop together at the same time. You can be sure that he spent many long hours at the tape recorder to create this short, but to many people, fascinating piece.

Here are some experiments you can try with classroom instruments. You may find some sounds that are very unusual.

AUTOHARP

American composer David Eddleman created an autoharp piece by caressing the strings with a chamois (SHA mee) cloth, brushing the strings with a comb, plucking individual strings between the fingernails, and drawing an eraser across the strings, often while strumming. An unusual effect is created by holding down two chord bars, one a minor chord and the other a corresponding major chord (G major and G minor, for example). The result is an open fifth— like a triad, but with the third left out. Listen to *Autoharp Fantasy*.

 Autoharp Fantasy............................Eddleman

MALLET INSTRUMENTS

Put the mallets in each hand and play tone clusters (notes that are right next to one another, like C, D, and E) on xylophone, glockenspiel, or metallophone. Vary your mallets. Use a tennis ball or the eraser end of a pencil.

RESONATOR BELLS

With the bells in their case, lean close to them and sing any pitches. You will hear the bells responding. Sing your name into the bells, with long pauses between syllables—*Jess-* (pause) *-i-* (pause) *-ca* (pause)—and listen as the bells respond to your speaking voice. This effect will work even better using a piano with the damper pedal depressed.

PIANO

Take a ruler or your forearm and depress a whole cluster of keys. (Alternate between black key clusters and white key clusters.) Our friend John Cage startled the musical world some years ago by writing a piece for "prepared piano." The piano was prepared by placing various articles on the felts, or against the strings to alter the sound. Listen to *Dance,* for prepared piano. Do you think it still sounds like a piano?

 Dance...Cage

Melody

So far, you would think all twentieth-century composers went out of their way to create new sounds. Not so. In 1917, Prokofiev wrote a symphony in the style of Mozart and Haydn (Remember them?). He called it *Classical Symphony* because he wanted to suggest the form and character of the late eighteenth-century symphony. Of course, it isn't exactly in the same style, because Prokofiev used melodic and harmonic styles that could only be from the twentieth century, with their sharp melodic turns and harmonic dissonances. Listen to the "Gavotte" from the *Classical Symphony,* and follow the line score.

Classical Symphony, Movement 3, "Gavotte"... Prokofiev

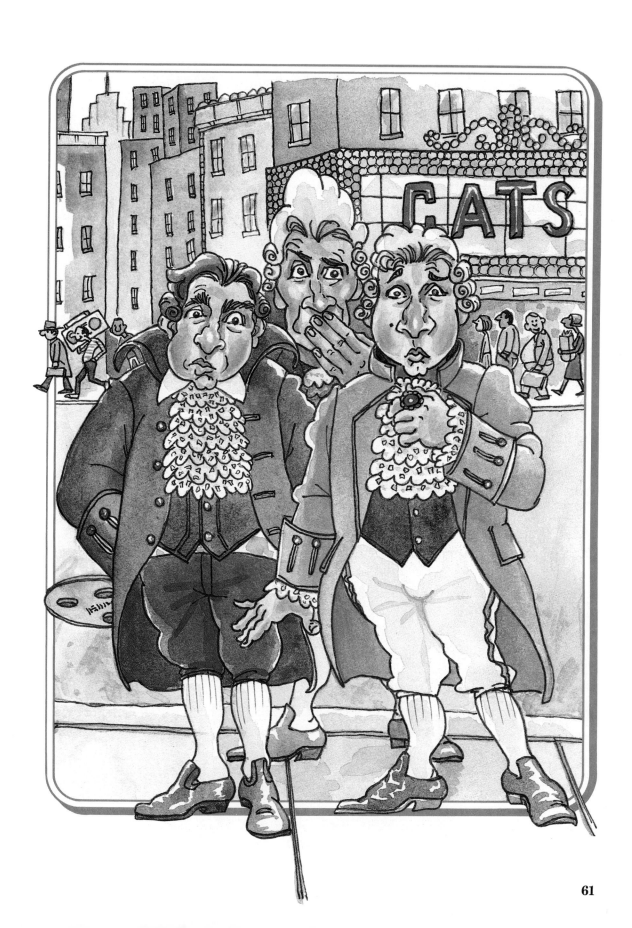

61

Melody, Melody, Who Has the Melody?

The melody in the "Gavotte" *might* be considered singable, but you would have a hard time singing it. The extreme range from top note to bottom, as well as the fragment with leaps, would make it a difficult singing piece.

Melodies of the twentieth century are hard to pin down. Some of them are singable in the old nineteenth-century way. Others are so untraditionally melodic that they are difficult to follow. In these pieces that feature the flute, what kinds of melodies do you hear?

Listening for Melodic Styles
Interpolations for Flute (excerpt) . . . Haubenstock-Ramati

Irlandaise (excerpt) . . . . Bolling

Opus Vetrinus (excerpt) . . . . Eddleman and Roberts

Sonata for Flute, Movement 2 (excerpt) . . . . Hindemith

Or (excerpt) . . . . Dick

The flutist in the pictures could be playing each piece, but what does the graphic suggest about the melody?

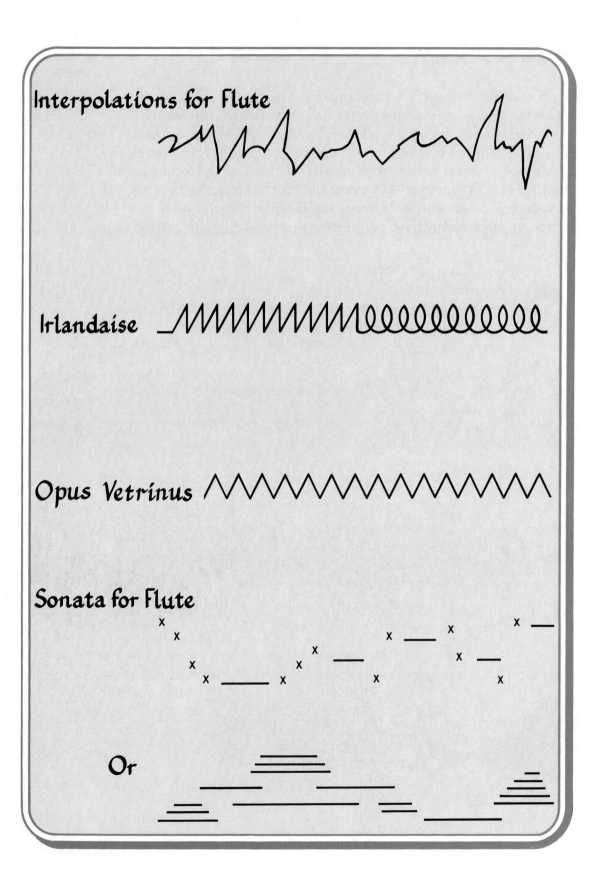

Interpolations for Flute

Irlandaise

Opus Vetrinus

Sonata for Flute

Or

Rhythms Today

It may be that the rhythm practices of the twentieth century will be known as the most revolutionary of its innovations. Through the centuries, a slow and gradual development of melody and harmony took place, but not even the new harmonic language of the twentieth century could equal the burst of activity in rhythm. Listen to part of the finale of Stravinsky's 1913 work *The Rite of Spring* to hear the way the composer constantly keeps the listener off balance by shifting meters and playing *polyrhythms* (several rhythms played at the same time).

The Rite of Spring, "Finale" (excerpt)........Stravinsky

Many composers followed Stravinsky's lead. They wrote in ever more complicated rhythmic styles. It finally took the computer to be able to realize some of these composers' complex rhythmic ideas.

The simple percussion piece notated below shows some of the ways a composer might vary an uncomplicated rhythm. In this example $\frac{4}{4}$ ♩ ♫ ♩ ♩ | is subjected to certain changes. Yet the resulting new rhythms still retain the basic character of the original rhythm.

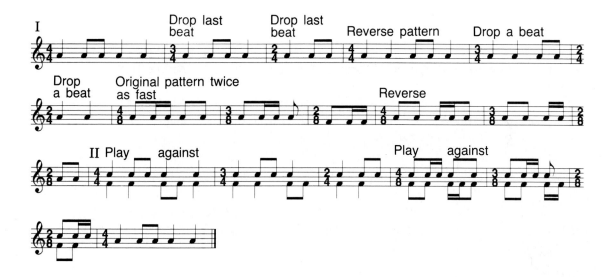

Here is how to play the percussion piece:

- Choose a percussion instrument to play all the measures in a meter of 4.

- Choose a different percussion instrument to play all the measures in a meter of 3.

- Choose a third instrument to play all the measures in a meter of 2.

- In Section II, percussion players play the bottom part and everyone else chants the rhythms on *cha*.

- Everyone performs in the last measure.

Harmony—Wild and Wacky

Listen to these two short pieces for piano. One is by Beethoven, a Classic composer. The other is by Béla Bartók, a twentieth-century composer. As you listen, ask yourself how the harmonies differ.

 Minuet in G . . . . Beethoven

 Mikrokosmos, "Wrestling" . . . . Bartók

Could you hear that the harmony in the Beethoven piece was different than the harmony in the Bartók piece? When you listened to *The Rite of Spring* in the previous lesson, you heard some fairly unusual harmonies there as well. In the twentieth century, harmony, like every other element of music, evolved into something very different from what it had been in the preceding centuries. Many people are repelled by the new harmonies; others find them exciting and stimulating. Whatever your own feeling, harmony will never be the same after the experiments of the twentieth century.

In the 1940s, Elliott Carter, a twentieth-century American composer, wrote a piece on a *single* chord for flute, oboe, clarinet, and bassoon. Listen to what Carter did with the chord.

 Etudes for Woodwind Quartet, No. 3 . . . . Carter

Tone Clusters

Elliott Carter used one D-major chord as material for an entire composition. Other composers use chords of many notes. Some even use chords that have every note. Do you remember the tone clusters mentioned on page 59?

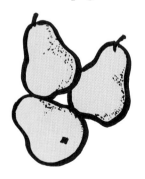

Try this. Take a ruler and depress as many piano keys as you can. Use the lower pitches of the piano. Charles Ives used this technique in his composition *Majority*. Notice how the cluster is notated.

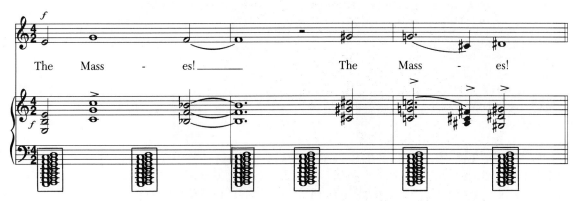

By Charles Ives. Reproduced by permission of the publisher.

The Polish composer Krzysztof Penderecki (KREESH tohf pehn deh REHT skee) used string clusters in his piece *Threnody for the Victims of Hiroshima.* Listen to the piece and examine the last page from the score. You can see the big blocks that stand for the tone clusters in this all-strings work.

Threnody for the Victims of Hiroshima .... **Penderecki**

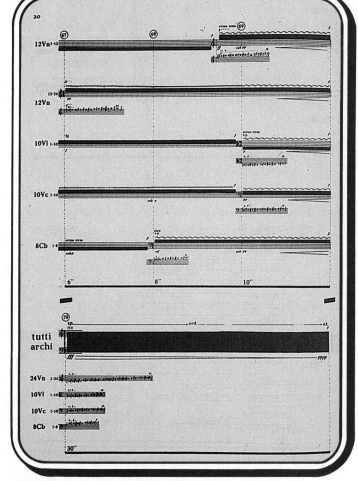

by Penderecki. Copyright © 1961 by Deshon Music, Inc. and PWM Editions. Used with permission. All Rights Reserved.

Whatever You Do, Don't Pull the Plug!

The synthesizer! Who hasn't heard it? It bleeps forth from almost every rock group. From Kool and the Gang to the Eurythmics, the synthesizer has been an indispensable instrument. Curiously enough, this instrument—able to recreate the sound of any traditional instrument as well as to create brand-new sounds—found favor at first with "serious" composers. They manipulated the basic wave forms produced by the machine and created musical compositions, some of great length. Listen to some of the wave forms the synthesizer manufactures.

Wave Forms
  (a) Sine wave (low)—very pure sound
  (b) Sine wave (high)—very pure sound
  (c) Sawtooth wave—a nasal sound
  (d) White noise—not a wave form, but all frequencies
      sounding at one time. It sounds like a hiss

Call Chart 5

Listen to a piece that uses these wave forms. You will hear how Raaijmakers (RYE mah kehrs) alters them to create organization and interest. Follow the Call Chart to help you listen more clearly.

 4 *Contrasts* (Part 2) .... Raaijmakers

1	INTRODUCTION	Filtered white noise in syncopated rhythm
2	SECTION A	Filtered white noise sweeping and popping in random sequence and bouncing back and forth from speaker to speaker, a low-pitched sine wave accompanies; later joined by higher pitched sine wave using a little "slide."
3	SECTION B	Increased activity of white noise pops and sweeps accompanied by a sawtooth wave ↗ ↘; syncopated white noise from introduction returns
4	SECTION A	Similar to call 2
5	CODA	Low-pitched sine wave with sawtooth wave ↗ ↘

Sound crazy? Not really. Raaijmakers has given us a piece that is thoroughly worked out. It has been said that "the sky's the limit," and this is surely true of twentieth-century music. Listen to this piece from a suite by Gustav Holst. He wrote it in 1916 (think of Stravinsky and what *he* was doing about that time). The suite is called *The Planets* and is a musical description of all the planets in the solar system except Earth and as-yet-undiscovered Pluto. Our selection is "Mercury," the "winged messenger." Isn't it amazing that the Stravinsky piece, the Raaijmakers piece, and the Holst piece are all products of our own century?

 4 *The Planets,* "Mercury" .... Holst

Getting a Good Blend

Men and women have probably sung together in groups since people first developed music. That kind of group singing was probably only in unison, with all voices singing the same thing at the same time.

Our "modern" tradition of choral singing in many parts came out of the medieval church, in which men (and sometimes boys with unchanged voices) sang the service chants in unison. These chants—known as plainsongs, plainchants, or Gregorian chants (for Pope Gregory the Great, who lived from about 540 to 604)—had only one purpose: to point up the meaning of the religious text. Their "otherworldly" quality truly captured the mystery and sense of religious awe as practiced by the medieval church.

Listen to this plainsong selection. Can you hear how the voices blend, almost as if the men were singing with one voice? Look at the notation on page 71. It looks very different from our modern-day notation. The little square notes are called *neumes*. Can you follow the neumes as you listen? (You can sing "Gaudeamus." The song is printed in modern notation on page 259.)

Gaudeamus omnes in Domino (excerpt)........ Plainsong

"Old Hundred"

"Old Hundred" has been sung in the United States since the
Puritans brought it over in 1628 in a book called *Whole Book of
Psalms.*

Just as the monks blended their voices in the plainsong selection,
try blending your voices as you sing "Old Hundred." Listen to your
neighbor and try to match your voice to his or hers. Or as one
teacher often puts it, "try to sing with the voice of the person next
to you."

Old Hundred

Words by William Kethe   Music by Louis Bourgeois

1. All peo - ple that on earth do dwell,
2. Oh, en - ter then His gates with praise,

Sing to the Lord with cheer - ful voice;
Ap - proach with joy His courts un - to;

Him serve with fear, His praise forth tell;
Praise, laud, and bless His name al - ways,

Come ye be - fore Him and re - joice.
For it is seem - ly so to do.

You should have performed this song *a cappella* (without
accompaniment). Did you stay on pitch, or did your pitch rise (go
sharp) or fall (go flat)? It is necessary to listen carefully all the time
when singing *a cappella* to be sure to stay on pitch.

Monophonic and Polyphonic Textures

Do you see a connection between the melody of "Old Hundred" and this diagram?

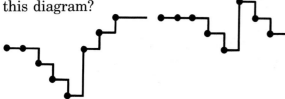

If you recognized the outline of "Old Hundred," you were right. And since there is only one line of music, we call it *monophony* or *monophonic texture*. Monophony sounds like a ten-dollar word until you break it down—mono (one) phonic (from the Greek word *phones*, pronounced FOH nays, meaning "voice"), or one voice. The Gregorian chant, as well as "Old Hundred," is an example of monophonic texture.

As time progressed, musicians began to add other voices to the single-line plainchants. Usually, in the eleventh or twelfth centuries, the extra voices just sang the melody at a higher or lower interval. "Old Hundred," if it had been written then, would have looked like this in our graph.

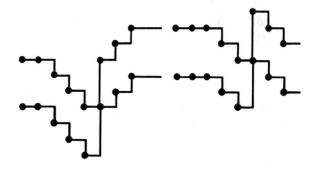

This kind of texture took a new name. We call it *polyphonic*—from poly (many) phonic (again, from the Greek *phones*—"voice")—or many-voiced music. Listen to the way this kind of music sounds.

Rex caeli, Domine . . . . Ninth century polyphony

Creative composers found this note-against-note writing to be limiting. Eventually a new style of polyphonic choral writing developed. In this new style, each voice was independent and had a different melody from the other voices. Yet each voice contributed to the whole piece. The voices were independent, yet they were written so that they had no complete meaning without the other voices. Listen to the example of polyphonic music on the following pages and see if you can follow the vocal lines as they progress through the piece.

Kyrie

Words Traditional   Music by Antonio Lotti

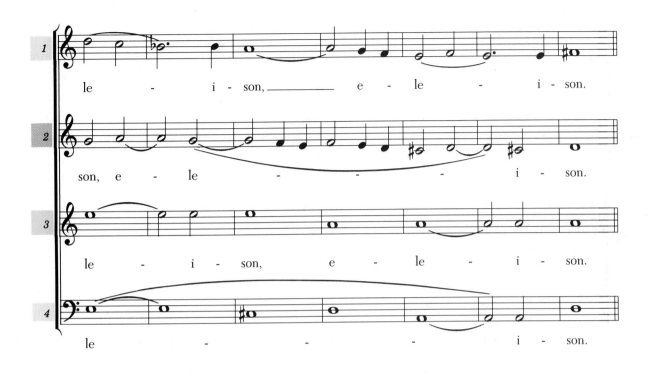

le   -   i - son, ——— e - le   -   i - son.

son, e - le   -   -   i - son.

le   -   i - son,   e - le - i - son.

le   -   -   -   i - son.

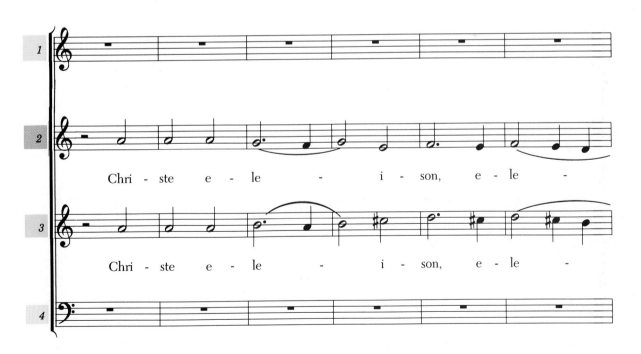

Chri - ste e - le   -   i - son, e - le -

Chri - ste e - le   -   i - son, e - le -

75

Developing Breath Control

Most rounds that you sing are in polyphonic texture. The round below has many long phrases. You have to have good breath control to sing them! Your teacher will explain some good ways to get from one end of these lengthy phrases to the other end. You will occasionally see a comma (') above the music. The comma shows you where to take a breath. In the entire round there are only *two* breath marks.

The Hunter

Traditional

The hunt-er winds his bu-gle horn, __ To horse! To horse! Hel-lo, Hel-lo! __ The fier-y cours-ers snuff the morn __ While throng-ing serf __ and lord pur-sue. The ea-ger pack in cou-ples freed __ Dash through the brook, the briar, the brake, __ While an-s'ring horn and hound and steed __ The for-est ech-oes star-tling wake. Up springs from yon-der tan-gled thorn A deer more white than moun-tain snow; __ While loud-er rings the hunt-er's horn, Hark! For-ward! For-ward! Hel-lo! Hel-lo!

Homophonic Texture

This chorale shows a different kind of texture. Here all the voices sing basically the same rhythm, with different notes for each voice. This kind of harmony is called *homophony* (hah MAH foh nee, meaning "same voice"), or *homophonic texture*. Even when one or two voices sing smaller notes, the other voices go on with the same rhythm. This hymn-like setting is placed on a *grand staff*—two staffs joined by a brace or bracket with treble clef for the top staff and bass clef for the bottom.

The King of Love My Shepherd Is

Psalm 23, from the *Scottish Psalter*   Irish Folk Melody   Harmonized by Daffyd Dylan

1. The king of love my shep-herd is, Whose good-ness fail-eth nev-er; I noth-ing lack if I am his And he is mine for-ev-er.

2. Where streams of liv-ing wa-ter flow, My ran-somed soul he lead-eth, And where the ver-dant pas-tures grow with food ce-les-tial feed-eth.

3. And so through all the length of days Thy good-ness fail-eth nev-er; Good shep-herd, may I sing thy praise with-in thy house for-ev-er.

Singing Partner Songs

Sometimes a song can be sung at the same time as another song. These partner songs can be fun to sing and will produce a type of polyphony that sounds different from some polyphonic music that you have heard or sung.

Learn to sing this song.

We're All Together Again

Traditional

Used by permission of the Boy Scouts of America.

When you have learned "We're All Together Again," learn to sing "While Strolling Through the Park" on the next page. After you have learned it, you can sing the songs together as partner songs.

While Strolling Through the Park

Words and Music by Ed Haley

While ___ stroll - ing through the park one day, _____ In the
I im - med - i - ate - ly raised my hat, _____ And ___

mer - ry, mer - ry month of May, _____ I was tak - en by sur -
fi - nal - ly ___ she re - marked. ___ "I ___ nev - er shall for -

prise by a pair of ro - guish eyes, In a mo - ment my poor heart was stole a -
get that ___ love - ly af - ter - noon." I ___ met her at the foun - tain in the

way. _____ A smile ___ was all ___ she gave to me,
park. _____

D.C. al Fine

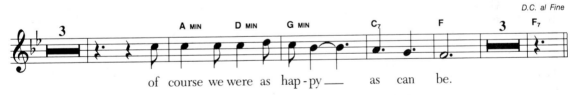

of course we were as hap - py ___ as can be.

The Oratorio

Have you ever heard *Messiah,* by George Frideric Handel? The "Hallelujah" chorus is one of its best-known sections.

Messiah is an *oratorio*—a musical drama a little like an opera, but usually without costumes, scenery, or stage action. Unlike in opera, audiences usually do not applaud after each aria or chorus in an oratorio. They listen quietly and may applaud at the end. Handel, as well as many other composers, wrote a great number of oratorios. His oratorio *Judas Maccabaeus* is the story of the Maccabean struggle to rid Palestine of its Syrian oppressors. Listen to a chorus from *Judas Maccabaeus.* It uses all the textures that you have studied—monophonic, homophonic, and polyphonic. Can you recognize them?

 Handel: *Judas Maccabaeus,* "Hallelujah, Amen"

Singing as a Group

You have practiced several singing techniques. Now, with your classmates, perform this song in unison as a choral group. Be aware of vocal blend ("singing with the voice of the person next to you"), watch diction and pitch, and try to exercise good breath control.

Dedication

English Version by Georg von Sudland   Music by Robert Franz

O, thank me not for songs I sing here, No gift of mine, they are your own. Yours was the gift, And I re-turn it, re-turn these songs to you a-lone. These songs were al-ways your pos-ses-sion, they sprang fresh from out your shin-ing eyes; There's where I heard them, there's where I learned them. Did you not know that each song is your own? Did you not know that each song is your own?

Singing in Parts

Singing successfully in parts, as you did in "The Fiddler," is a sign of musical independence. If you can "hold" your vocal part against someone else's different vocal part, it means you have developed a good ear and a good sense of harmony. Learn this part song. You might want to sing it in a concert sometime!

Water Come a Me Eye

Folk Song from Jamaica

1. Ev - 'ry time I 'mem - ber Li - za,
2. Since you gone the days are lone - ly, Wa - ter come a me eye,
3. When you here the time goes fast,

When I think 'bout my gal Li - za,
Come back gal, I love you on - ly, Wa - ter come a me eye.
Now you gone and love is past,

REFRAIN
Come back, Li - za, come back, gal, Wa - ter come a me eye.

Come back, Li - za, come back, gal, Wa - ter come a me eye.

A German Folk Song

The German composer Johannes Brahms loved to make arrangements of German folk songs. This one can be sung as a choral song in two parts. Work out each part separately, then put them together.

The Fiddler

English Version by Ruth Martin   Music by Johannes Brahms

1. A red beard-ed fid - dler who lived on the Rhine
2. "You red beard-ed fid - dler, now play us a tune,
3. The fid - dler struck up with his bow on the string,

Was walk - ing one night 'round a quar - ter to nine,
And we shall re - ward you both rich - ly and soon.
The la - dies danced round and___ round in a ring,

And___ on his way home, just guess___ what he saw, Just guess what he saw,
Bet - ter play us a dance that's mer - ry and light, That's mer - ry and light,
Then they all cried_ out with one_ ac - cord, With one ac - cord,

Not one___ pret - ty la - dy, but twen - ty or more!
For we___ have to cel - e - brate Wal - pur - gis night."
"You've fid - dled so well___ you shall have___ your re - ward."

4. And while all the ladies applauded and cheered,
One brought out a scissors and cut off his beard.
"We've paid for your tune far more than it's worth,
Far more than it's worth,
We've made you the handsomest fiddler on earth!"

What Do You Hear 1

 Afro-Amero . . . . Faini

Listen to the recording and as each number is called circle the correct answer.

1. Strong rhythm only　　　　　No rhythm alternates with strong rhythm

2. Fast tempo　　　　　Slow tempo

3. Loud, then soft　　　　　Soft only

4. Timpani　　　　　Flute

5. Tom-toms lead to short patterns　　Long flowing melody

6. Melody is slower　　　　　Melody gets faster

7. Complete silence　　　　　Strong irregular rhythm pattern

8. Melody much slower　　　　　Melody even faster

9. Polyrhythms　　　　　Only one rhythm on one instrument

10. Melody faster yet　　　　　Melody very slow and soft

86

Test 1

Write the letter of the correct answer in the blank.

1. One of the qualities of African music is _____ .
   a. violins
   b. harpsichords
   c. complex rhythm patterns
   d. electronic effects

2. A rhythm complex consists of _____ .
   a. several melodies sung together
   b. several rhythms played together
   c. a complicated rhythm pattern
   d. fear of rhythm

3. Two or more rhythms played at the same time are called _____ .
   a. polyrhythms
   b. percussion
   c. countermelodies
   d. snare drums

4. The Yoruba group worshiped a household god called _____ .
   a. Zeus
   b. Neptune
   c. Baal
   d. Elegua

5. African singers, as well as black American folk singers tend to _____ the melody.
   a. play
   b. write down
   c. ornament
   d. forget

Circle T if the statement is true; circle F if the statement is false.

6. Latin-American rhythms are less African than those in North America.

T   F

Test 2 ✓

Circle T if the statement is true; circle F if the statement is false.

1. Jazz is a blend of African rhythms and Western harmonies.

T   F

2. Improvisation is a European, not an African style.

T   F

3. A riff is a jazz name for an ostinato.

T   F

4. In jazz, players improvise over a predetermined chord scheme.

T   F

Write the letter of the correct answer in the blank.

5. Rhythmically, when strong emphasis is placed on something we expect to be weak, it is called _____ .

a. beat   b. a quarter note
c. meter   d. syncopation

6. Xylophones, marimbas, tom-toms, maracas, claves, slit drums, and conga drums are all _____ .

a. string instruments   b. percussion instruments
c. brass instruments   d. woodwind instruments

Test 3 ✓

Circle the letters next to the correct answer.

1. What is *style*?
   a. a large hat
   b. a beautiful house
   c. the appearance of an object; the way it looks
   d. a haircut

2. A period of musical history usually has music written in basically the same style. One period is given below. Which is it?
   a. Baroque
   b. Jazz
   c. Songs
   d. Rock and Roll

3. Mozart was a Classic composer; Schoenberg composed during what period?
   a. the Classic period
   b. the twentieth century
   c. The Renaissance period
   d. the Baroque period

4. The music of the Classic period is clean, clear, and harmonious. How, generally, might you describe the style of the twentieth century?
   a. melodic
   b. harmonically traditional
   c. dissonant
   d. rhythmically square

Write the letter of the correct answer in the blank.

5. The Classic period has also been called The Age of Enlightenment and the _____ .
   a. Age of Rocks
   b. Age of Reason
   c. Age of Aquarius
   d. Age of Gold

6. In Classic art, as well as music, there is a great deal of attention to _____ .
   a. three
   b. colors
   c. singing
   d. proportion and balance

7. In the song "In the Army," two like sections are separated by an unlike section. This is called _____ .
   a. rondo form
   b. a symphony
   c. ABA
   d. a piano

8. Beethoven was greatly influenced by _____ .
   a. the American Revolution
   b. the Thirty Years War
   c. the Mexican Revolution
   d. the French Revolution

Test 4 ✓

Circle T if the statement is true; circle F if the statement is false.

1. The Romantic period gave more importance to individual expression.

T   F

2. Franz Liszt was the first performer to give solo concerts.

T   F

3. Johannes Brahms was a good friend of Mozart.

T   F

4. *Sprechstimme* is a vocal technique that is part speech, part song.

T   F

Write the letter of the correct answer in the blank.

5. A type of notation that "draws pictures" of the kind of sound a performer should make is called _____ .
a. style notation   b. classic notation
c. graphic notation   d. scribbles

6. In *The Rite of Spring* Stravinsky wrote many rhythms to be played at the same time. This is called _____ . (Hint: You had this one in your study of African music.)
a. synthesizer   b. polyrhythm
c. tape recorder   d. multimeter

7. In *Threnody for the Victims of Hiroshima,* Penderecki uses lots of notes close together called _____ .
a. polyrhythm   b. melodies
c. saxophones   d. tone clusters

8. A synthesizer creates sound by manipulating _____ .
a. wave forms   b. wave lengths
c. wave bands   d. wave fronts

Test 5 ✓

Circle the correct answer.

1. An ancient religious vocal form, sung in unison and notated in neumes.

          plainsong   art song   opera

2. What this kind of unison singing is called.

          monophonic   polyphonic

3. Adding a second voice at a different interval.

          polyphonic   voices

4. Many rounds are good examples of it.

          monophony   polyphony   atonality

5. Two or more voices singing the same rhythms, as in a hymn.

          monophony   polyphony   homophony

6. Two or more songs that will work when sung together.

          art songs   partner songs   cowboy songs

7. A musical drama, usually with a great deal of choral work, but with no costumes, scenery, or stage action.

          opera   musical comedy   cantata   oratorio

8. In singing, careful attention to the clear pronunciation of the text.

          dynamics   interpretation   diction

UNDERSTANDING MUSIC

Chapter 4—The Elements of Music

Melody

When you think of music, what do you think of first? If you are like most people, you probably think first of *melody*. Have you ever found yourself leaving a concert or a musical play whistling or humming the tunes you just heard? Have you ever thought about a television show or a movie just because you recognized its theme song? When you did those things, you were responding to the melody, the element that usually most identifies a piece of music.

During the fifteenth century a famous castle in Wales—Harlech Castle, seen on page 94—came under siege. This song commemorates that battle. As you sing "Men of Harlech," pay attention to the way the melody flows upward and downward.

Men of Harlech

English Version by William Duthie   Traditional Welsh Song

Melody *Steps* Out

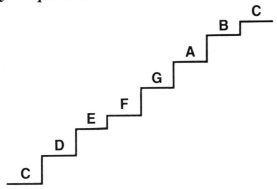

Melodies move in three different ways. They move by step when they are moving along the *scale*. What is a scale? Look at this example of a scale starting on the note C.

Each one of these notes is a step away from the note on either side. They move from a line to the next space to the next line to the next space, and so forth. As long as the notes move from a line to the next space or from a space to the next line, the melody is moving by step.

Listen to these examples of melodies moving by step.

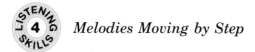

Melodies Moving by Step

On page 97 you will find a song that moves mostly by step. The basic idea repeats over and over. When the song leaves the step pattern, it can create a real surprise to the ears.

One of Those Songs

English Words by Will Holt   Music by Gerard Calvi

Melody *Leaps* About

Look at this scale passage. All the notes are moving by step. Play the passage on bells or on the piano.

C B A G F E D C

Now let's remove the notes shown in gray. Play the example on bells or piano leaving out the gray notes.

C A G E C

Do you hear the *leaps* in this passage? When notes move from one line to another line (or further) or from one space to another space (or further), we call this "movement by *leap*." Listen to these examples of melodies moving by leap.

 Melodies Moving by Leap

Skip to My Lou

Lou, Lou, skip to my Lou, Lou, Lou, skip to my Lou; Lou, Lou, skip to my Lou, skip to my Lou, my dar-ling.

The Star-Spangled Banner

Oh, __ say can you see, by the dawn's ear - ly light, What so proud - ly we hailed at the

twi-light's last gleam-ing.

98

"The Marine's Hymn" is the official song of the United States Marine Corps. Notice how the many leaps in the melody seem to suggest an energy that moving by step would not.

The Marine's Hymn

Traditional

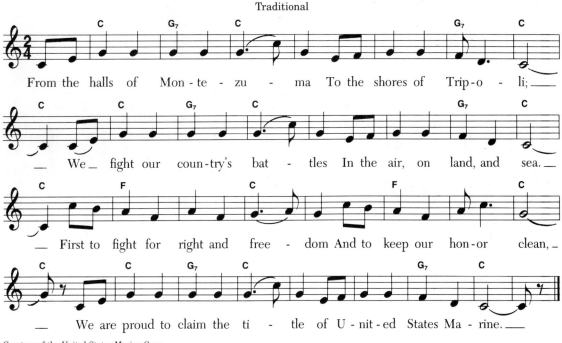

From the halls of Mon-te-zu - ma To the shores of Trip-o - li; __

__ We_ fight our coun-try's bat - tles In the air, on land, and sea. __

__ First to fight for right and free - dom And to keep our hon-or clean, __

__ We are proud to claim the ti - tle of U - nit-ed States Ma - rine. __

And Finally (We Repeat), Notes Repeat

Melody notes can repeat—just stay where they are. Look at the way "Old Abram Brown" begins—with a series of nine notes all the same.

Old Abram Brown

Words from "Tom Tiddler's Ground" by Walter de la Mare   Music by Benjamin Britten

I D MIN   II

Old   A - bram Brown is   dead and gone, We'll nev - er see him more.

III   IV

He used to wear an old gray coat All but - toned down be - fore.

All Steps Are Not Created Equal

Look at this drawing of a set of steps. Do you see anything peculiar about it?

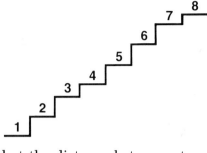

Did you notice that the distance between steps 3 and 4 and between 7 and 8 is not as great as the distance between the other steps? What kind of staircase is this? If you tried running up or down it, you'd probably trip!

Actually this is a musical staircase—a scale. Do you remember the one on page 96? If you play the scale, you might notice that the size of the steps is not always the same. Some steps are whole steps and others are half steps. Here is a scale on E♭ with the whole steps and half steps shown. Play the whole and half steps to hear their special "sound."

⌣ or ⌐ = whole step ∨ or ∧ = half step

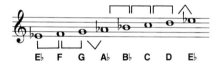

"Hello, My Baby" uses both whole steps and half steps. You can see some of the whole and half steps marked. Can you find others?

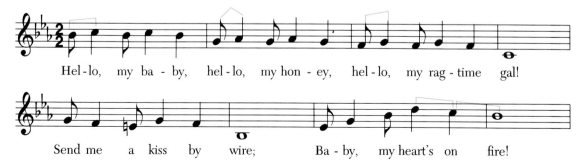

Hel-lo, my ba-by, hel-lo, my hon-ey, hel-lo, my rag-time gal!

Send me a kiss by wire; Ba-by, my heart's on fire!

If you re-fuse me, hon-ey, you'll lose me. Then you'll be left a-

lone; Oh, ba - by, tel - e - phone and tell me I'm your ___

|1. own. Hel - lo! Hel - lo! Hel - lo there!

|2. own! ___

Step to the Piano, Maestro

The piano keyboard is especially handy for showing whole steps and
half steps. Look at this keyboard. Between every white key and
black key there is a half step. But look at notes B and C and notes
E and F. There is no black note separating them. That's because
there is already a natural half step between these notes.

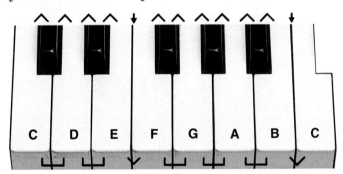

Now look at the frets on the fingerboard of this dulcimer. Can you
see that the frets are not the same size? Some are wider than
others. The wider frets are whole steps and the narrower ones are
half steps.

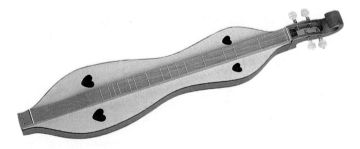

Scale Patterns—They Make a Difference

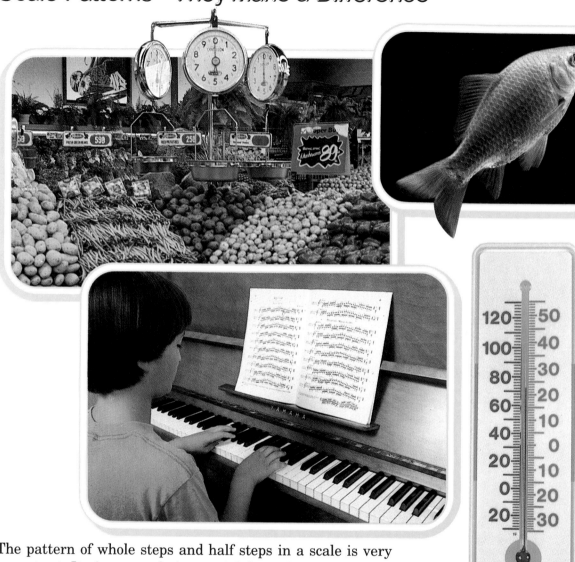

The pattern of whole steps and half steps in a scale is very important. It gives a scale its special "sound." The scales you have seen so far have all been *major* scales. A major scale has a step pattern of whole, whole, half, whole, whole, whole, half. As long as the pattern is followed, the scale will sound major no matter what note it begins on. That's why "Hello, My Baby" sounded as major as the scale on C. The scale still followed the major-scale pattern, even though it began on E♭.

Scale on E♭

E♭ F G A♭ B♭ C D E♭

Scale on C

C D E F G A B C

102

Key Signatures

A key signature is a kind of shorthand method to tell us what sharps (♯) or flats (♭) are needed to make the scale pattern conform to the whole step-half step pattern. Look at the E♭ scale again.

E♭ F G A♭ B♭ C D E♭

There are three flats needed to make the E♭ scale conform to the major-scale pattern. Since the flatted notes—E♭, A♭, and B♭—will appear each time, musicians simply gather those flats together and place them on the staff at the beginning of the line, like this:

That way the scale can be shown without writing flats all the time.

E♭ F G A♭ B♭ C D E♭

Here is a song in major key. It is in the key of C major. That means no sharps or flats are needed in the signature.

Merry Minstrels 5

Attributed to Henry Purcell

I
We mer - ry min-strels soft mu - sic en - joy, For mu - sic doth ha - tred and

II
mal - ice de - stroy. We sing so blithe - ly, we drive a - way care, And

III
with our soft har - mo - ny ban - ish de - spair. Then hail, sweet sci - ence, hail,

hail, heav'n - ly sound! No plea - sure like mu - sic on earth can be found.

The Minor Scale

Look at these two scales. The one on the left is a major scale on C.
The one on the right is a *minor* scale, also on C.

C major

C minor

Play the two scales up and down to hear their special sound. What
do you notice about their whole- and half-step patterns? The major-
scale pattern is W W H W W W H. The minor scale, however, has a
pattern of W H W W H W W.

"Hatikvah" is written on a minor scale based on D. It would look
like this. Notice the key signature. We say that this is the key of D
minor.

Hatikvah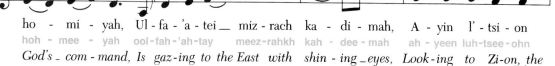
(Hope)

Hebrew Words by Naftali Herz Imber   English Words by David Eddleman
Traditional Hebrew Melody

Kol___ od ba - le - vav p' - ni - mah   Ne - fesh y' - hu - di
kohl   ohd bah - leh - vahv puh - nee - mah   neh - fehsh yuh - hoo - dee
Yearn - ing for free - dom in Zi - on's___ land,   Each He - brew soul, by

ho - mi - yah, Ul - fa - 'a - tei___ miz - rach ka - di - mah, A - yin l' - tsi - on
hoh - mee - yah ool - fah - 'ah - tay   meez - rahkh kah - dee - mah   ah - yeen luh - tsee - ohn
God's___ com - mand, Is gaz - ing to the East with shin - ing___ eyes, Look - ing to Zi - on, the

tso - fi - yah.   Od lo av - dah tik - va - te - nu,   Ha - tik - vah bat
tsoh - fee - yah   ohd loh ahv - dah teek - vah - tay - noo   hah - teek - vah baht
an - cient___ prize. 'Twas not lost, our hope___ so___ sure,   Through the a - ges

shnot al-pa-yim,
shnoht ahl-pah-yeem
did___ en-dure;

L'h'yot am chof-shi
luh-hee oht ahm khohf-shee
Free-dom a-gain, our

b'-ar-tsei-nu, b'-
buh-'ar-tsay-noo buh-
peo-ple___ yearned_ for the

e-rets Tsi-on v'y'-ru-sha-la-yim.
eh-rehts tsee-ohn vuh yuh-roo-shah-lah-yeem
land of Zi-on and Je-ru-sa-lem.

L'h'yot am chof-shi
luh hee oht ahm khohf-shee
Free-dom a-gain, our

b'-ar-tsei-nu, b'-e-rets tsi-on v'y'-ru-sha-la-yim.
buh-'ahr-tsay-noo buh-'eh-rehts tsee-ohn vuh yuh-roo-sha-lah-yeem
peo-ple___ yearned_ for the land of Zi-on and Je-ru-sa-lem.

Call Chart 6

Listen to this Call Chart. Some of the selections are in major keys; others are in minor keys.

1. *The Nutcracker,* "Chinese Dance" (excerpt).........Tchaikovsky
2. *L'Arlésienne,* "Prélude" (excerpt) ....Bizet
3. *Sinfonietta,* Movement 1 (excerpt) ....Janácek
4. *Peer Gynt,* "In the Hall of the Mountain King" (excerpt)....Grieg
5. *The Water Music,* "Allegro" (excerpt) ....Handel

Some songs begin in minor and go to major. This song is one of them. Can you tell when the melody changes to major and when it returns to minor? (You will find this song notated on page 300.)

Time in a Bottle.....................................Croce

That Ol' Split-Level Scale

Both the major and minor scales have a pattern of whole steps and half steps within the eight-note scale. (Actually there are only seven notes. The eighth is the same note as the first note, only it is an *octave* [eight tones] above the beginning note. These two notes have the same letter name.) If you have ever listened to any folk music or even to certain popular music, you may have heard a different kind of scale—a scale consisting of only *five* notes. Beginning on C, it would look like this.

Do you see the space between E and G? That gap of one and a half steps has sometimes caused this scale to be called a *gapped* scale. Actually its real name is the *pentatonic* (*penta-*, "five"; *tonic,* "toned") scale. Play the scale up and down on bells or piano to hear its special sound. Notice that there are no half steps (unless you consider the one and a half steps between E and G). Here is another pentatonic scale, this time on G.

Play the pentatonic scale on G up and down. Except for its different position, it sounds the same as the pentatonic scale on C. That is because the two scales share the same pattern of whole steps and the gap of one and a half steps.

In this song the first part of the melody, marked A, is based on the pentatonic scale you just played. The second part, marked B, goes to the major scale, but it uses only *five* of the notes of the major scale—F$\sharp$, G, A, B, and C. That way there is a five-note correspondence between section A and section B. Can you hear the difference as you sing?

I'd Like to Teach the World to Sing

Words and Music by Bill Backer, Billy Davis, Roger Cook and Roger Greenaway
Arrangement by David Fiorenza and Daniel Shigo

And Now for a Brief Interval

In a melody a leap is a leap. Right? Well, yes and no. A leap or a step is also an *interval,* and a specific kind of interval at that! Look at this interval. Play it or sing it to hear its sound.

This interval is called a *third.* Why? Let's look at this third interval more closely.

If you start with the lower note of the interval and count up by *lines and spaces* to the higher note, the number you place on the higher note will tell you its interval, in this case, a third. Look at these intervals. Can you tell what they are by counting the lines and spaces?

On page 109 the song "You're Never Fully Dressed Without a Smile" contains many intervals of different widths. Can you name the intervals in the brackets?

You're Never Fully Dressed Without a Smile

from *Annie*

Words by Martin Charnin   Music by Charles Strouse

Hey, ho - bo man, Hey, Dap - per Dan, You both got your
Your clothes may be Beau Brum - el - ly, They stand out a

style,
mile, } But bro - ther, You're nev - er ful - ly dressed with - out a

1. smile!
2. smile! Who cares what they're

wear - ing on Main Street or Sa - vile Row? It's what you wear from ear to

ear, and not from head to toe that mat - ters; So, Sen - a - tor,

So, jan - i - tor, So long for a while, Re - mem - ber, you're

nev - er ful - ly dressed, though you may wear the best, You're

nev - er ful - ly dressed with - out a smile.

Melody—On Its Construction Site

What have you discovered so far? You have discovered that composers have quite a few melodic devices to help them build a melody. One was *repetition*. Listen to how these composers use repetition of phrases, motives, or notes to build a melody.

Melody Building
The Olympian (excerpt)............................Glass
Carmina Burana, "O Fortuna" (excerpt)...........Orff
Symphony No. 7 in A, Movement 2 (excerpt) ..Beethoven

What kind of repetition does the composer use in this song?

Just in Time

from *Bells Are Ringing*

Words by Betty Comden and Adolph Green　　Music by Jule Styne

Sequence

Do you know what a sequence is? You probably know that a sequence is a series of events or objects. In music, *sequence* has a very precise meaning. Look at this melodic example.

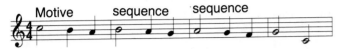

The first measure is a simple melodic idea called a *motive*. The next two measures have exactly the same pattern except that each one begins a step lower. That's a sequence, and it's a good tool for composers when they need to expand their material.

This song has many sequences. Learn to sing it and be aware of all the sequences.

Variation and Contrast

The apples in the picture represent a wide variety of this common fruit. The oranges, on the other hand, are a contrast to the apples. Oranges are quite different from apples.

Composers use variation and contrast to make their melodies interesting. Look at the melody of "This Old Hammer." See how the many melodic devices, including variation and contrast, make this melody "work."

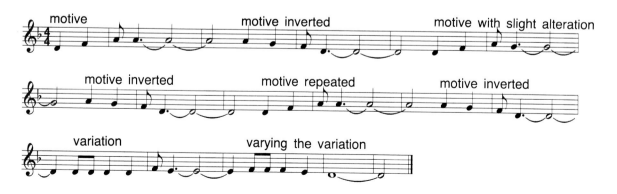

Add Rhythm to Move a Melody

Do you remember *Gaudeamus omnes in Domino* on page 70? It was an example of medieval plainsong and seemed to have no regular rhythm. The rhythm was created by the words. Every melody—even a seemingly nonrhythmic one like *Gaudeamus*—needs rhythm to give it shape and character. Look at this four-note motive, for example.

Now add rhythm and see what happens.

"One of Those Songs"   **"Chester"**

Look at "Row, Row, Row Your Boat." This simple round that you have probably sung all your life takes on a whole new character when the rhythm is changed.

Row, Row, Row Your Boat (5)

Traditional Round

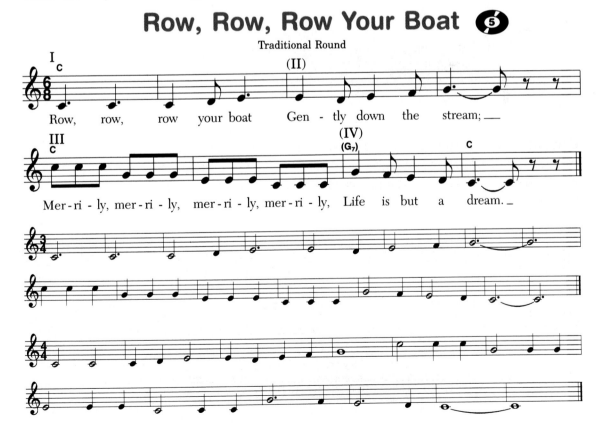

Clap a Rhythm, Call a Song!

On page 112 you saw a four-note motive and several rhythm patterns that helped identify the song. Now here is a short rhythm pattern. Can you name any songs that use this rhythm?

Now for the big event! Combine the rhythm pattern above with the note pattern on page 113 and sing . . .

This Land Is Your Land

Words and Music by Woody Guthrie   Countermelody by Ruth Tutelman

REFRAIN
Countermelody (sing last time only)

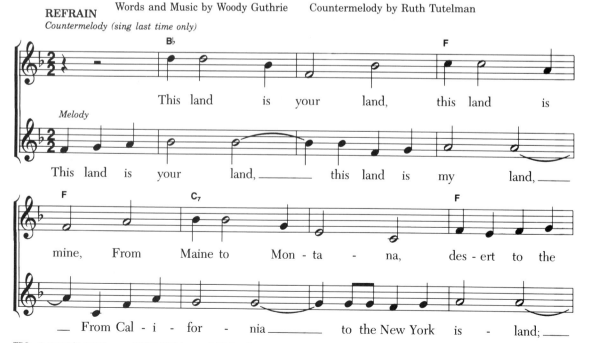

This land is your land, this land is

This land is your land, this land is my land,

mine, From Maine to Mon-ta-na, des-ert to the

From Cal-i-for-nia to the New York is-land;

shore, We sing that this land is your land, this land is

From the red-wood for - est _____ to the Gulf Stream wa - ters; _____

mine, Yes, it's made for you and me. _____

_____ This land was made for you and me. _____

VERSE

1. As I was walk - ing _____ that rib - bon of high - way, _____
2. I've roamed and ram - bled _____ and I fol-lowed my foot - steps _____
3. When the sun comes shin - ing _____ and I _____ was stroll - ing _____

_____ I saw a - bove me _____ that end - less sky - way, _____
_____ to the spar - kling sands of _____ her dia - mond des - erts, _____
_____ And the wheat - fields wav - ing _____ and the dust clouds roll - ing, _____

_____ I saw be - low me _____ that gold - en val - ley, _____
_____ And all a - round me _____ a voice was sound - ing, _____
_____ As the fog was lift - ing _____ a voice was chant - ing, _____

D.C. al Fine

_____ This land was made for you and me. _____
_____ "This land was made for you and me." _____
_____ "This land was made for you and me." _____

Beats in Groups

Meter in 2

What do you notice about these quarter notes?

There isn't much to notice is there? They're just plodding along. But what happens when we accent (>) every other one?

The beats are grouped in *twos*—a *meter in 2*. Musicians usually put *bar lines* between each grouping:

Look at the conducting pattern in $\frac{2}{4}$ meter. Try conducting some songs in this book that are in a meter of 2.

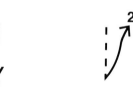

The Meter Signature

A meter needs a meter signature to tell the musicians what the meter grouping is and what note is going to represent the beat. The bottom number of the meter signature tells you what kind of note represents the beat; so $\frac{2}{8}$ means that the eighth note (♪) represents the beat and $\frac{2}{2}$ means that the half note ( ) represents the beat and $\frac{2}{4}$ means that the quarter note ( ) represents the beat. The key idea, however, is that if there is a top number 2, the meter is in 2 no matter what note represents the beat.

Meter in 4

Many songs in this book are in a meter of 4. They carry a meter signature of $\frac{4}{4}$. That means the beats are grouped in fours and a *quarter note* ( ) represents the beat. Look at the conducting pattern for a meter of 4.

On page 117 is a song in $\frac{4}{4}$ meter. Learn the conducting patterns and conduct that song or any other songs in a meter of 4 in your book.

The Rose

Words and Music by Amanda McBroom

1. Some say love, it is a riv - er that drowns ___ the ten - der ___ reed.

Some say love, it is a raz - or that leaves ___ your soul to ___ bleed.

Some say ___ love, ___ it is a hun - ger, an end - less ach - ing need. ___

I say ___ love, it is a flow - er, and you it's on - ly seed. ___

2. It's the ___ heart a - fraid of break - in' that nev - er ___ learns to ___ dance.
3. When the ___ night has been too lone - ly, and the road ___ has been too ___ long,

It's the ___ dream ___ a-fraid of wak - in' that nev - er ___ takes the ___ chance.
And you ___ think ___ that love is on - ly for the luck - y ___ and the ___ strong,

It's the ___ one ___ who won't be tak - en ___ who can - not seem to give, ___
Just re - mem - ber, ___ in ___ the win - ter, ___ far be - neath ___ the win - ter snows ___

1.

And the ___ soul a - fraid of dy - in', that nev - er ___ learns to live. ___
Lies the ___ seed that with the sun's ___ love, in the

2.

___

spring be - comes the rose. ___

Meter in 3

Listen to these recordings of waltzes. Can you feel that the beats are grouped in threes?

 Belle of the Ball . . . . Anderson
Masquerade Suite, **"Waltz"** (excerpt) . . . . . . Khachaturian

Look at the way these systems of numbers are now grouped in threes.

And if we place bar lines in the right places and add an appropriate meter signature, we are ready to conduct in 3!

Look at the conducting patterns. Try them out. They will help you feel the meter in 3. When you think you have practiced the conducting patterns for 3 enough, try conducting the song that begins below.

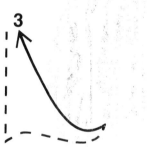

My White Horse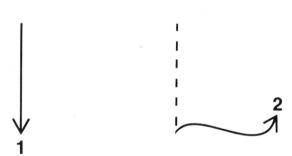
(Mi caballo blanco)

Words and Music by Francisco Flores del Campo   English Words by Samuele Maqui

My horse is like the sun - rise, __ My horse as white as dawn.
Es mi ca - ba - llo blan - co, __ Co - mo un a - ma - ne - cer,
ehs mee cah-bah-yoh blahn - koh coh-mohoon ah - mah - neh - sehr

We al - ways ride to - geth - er __ Sing - ing as we ride a - long.
Siem - pre jun - ti - tos va - mos, __ Es mia - mi - go mas fi - el.
syehm-preh hoon-tee-tohs vah - mohs ehs mehah-mee-goh mahs fee - ehl

Mi ca - ba - llo, mi ca - ba - llo, He's gal - lop - ing on, _____
mee cah-bah-yoh mee cah-bah-yoh Ga - lo - pan - do va, _____
gah-loh - pahn - doh vah

Mi ca - ba - llo, mi ca - ba - llo, in - to _____ the dawn.
mee cah-bah-yoh mee cah-bah-yoh se va_y_____ se va.
seh vah ee seh vah

Ah _____ Hmm. _____

119

Alternating 2 and 3 (A Neat Trick)

Many composers, especially those of the twentieth century, have been attracted to *multimeter,* a verbal mouthful that simply means "more than one meter in a composition." In this setting of "Tumbalalaika," the arranger has taken an old folk song and altered its meter to give it an unusual feeling. Notice that the first few measures are in $\frac{3}{4}$, and the *Tumbalalaika* words are set in $\frac{2}{2}$. The coda is the tricky part. Look at its meter signature. It is $\frac{3}{4}\frac{2}{4}$. That means the metric grouping changes with each measure—from $\frac{3}{4}$ to $\frac{2}{4}$ and back again.

Tumbalalaika

Jewish Folk Song   English Words by Margaret Fishback   Arranged by Lawrence Eisman

1. Pac - ing, puz - zling all the night long, A
2. "Maid - en, maid - en, can you ex - plain
3. "I - dle lad, you're jok - ing, I know. A

young lad sang a haunt - ing song.
What can grow with - out snow or rain?
stone can grow with - out rain or snow,

"What shall I say to my love to - day, Oh
What ____ can burn for end - less years, and
Love ____ can blaze and nev - er die, A

what shall I say to my love to - day?"
what ____ can cry and shed ____ no tears?"
heart ____ can weep and nev - er cry."

Tum - bal - a, tum - bal - a, tum - bal - a - lai - ka,

120

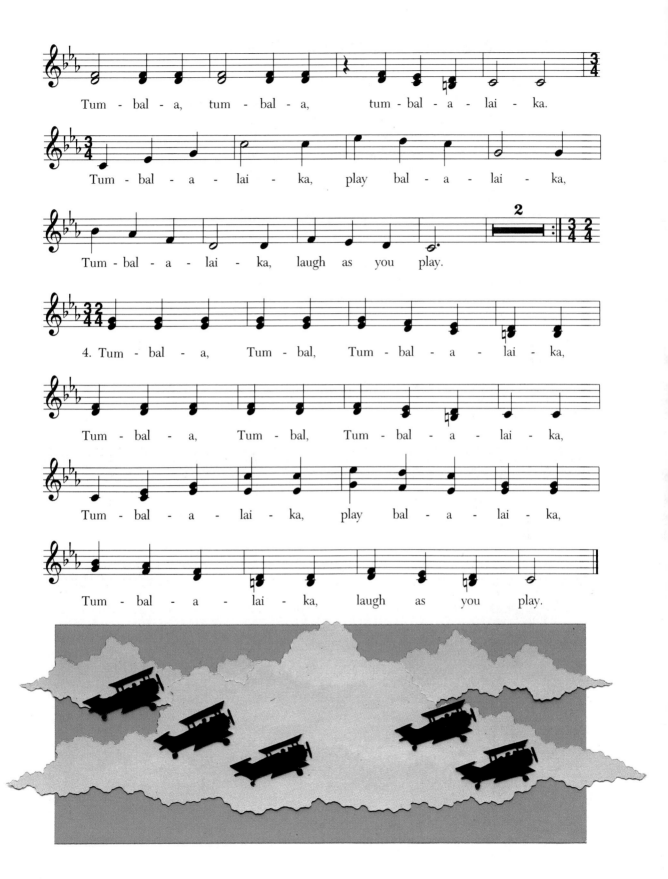

Tum - bal - a, tum - bal - a, tum - bal - a - lai - ka.

Tum - bal - a - lai - ka, play bal - a - lai - ka,

Tum - bal - a - lai - ka, laugh as you play.

4. Tum - bal - a, Tum - bal, Tum - bal - a - lai - ka,

Tum - bal - a, Tum - bal, Tum - bal - a - lai - ka,

Tum - bal - a - lai - ka, play bal - a - lai - ka,

Tum - bal - a - lai - ka, laugh as you play.

The Long and the Short of It

Sooner or later the time comes to talk seriously about notation. You may have had some study in musical notation before now, perhaps in a lower school grade; in band, orchestra, or chorus; or in private lessons. It is very hard to talk about music if you don't know at least the basics of notation. Here goes.

Basically, notes show how long they are to be held. They don't even need a staff to do that. When notes are introduced on a staff, their placement shows the *pitch* of the notes. (But you probably already know that.)

If you can divide by two, you can understand rhythmic notation. The largest unit of rhythmic notation is the *whole note*. o

The whole note (o) and every smaller note can be divided in half. So the whole note can be broken into two halves. o = ♩ ♩

And breaking down further we find . . .

half
notes quarter notes

♩ ♩ = ♩ ♩ ♩ ♩

quarter notes eighth notes

♩ ♩ ♩ ♩ = ♫ ♫ ♫ ♫

eighth notes   sixteenth notes

♫ ♫ ♫ ♫ = ♬♬ ♬♬ ♬♬ ♬♬

Do you notice how each note is named for its division from the whole note? That helps to figure out its relationship to all other notes.

Music's Triple Threat—The Triplet

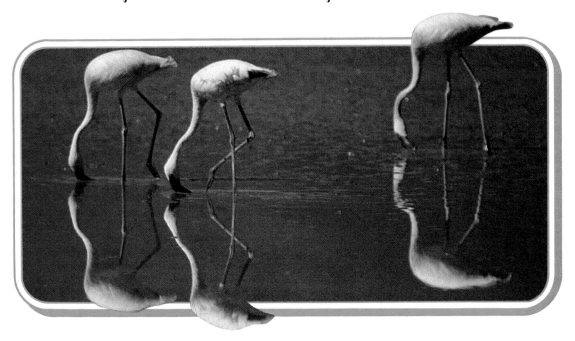

Do you see anything unusual in this song from *Oliver*? Follow it as you listen to the recording.

6 *Oliver!*, "Food, Glorious Food" (excerpt)............Bart

If you heard the rhythm ♪♪♪, you heard a *triplet*. Triplets are three equal notes spread over the space of two of the same value. Try clapping this rhythm to get the feel of triplets. It's simple!

124

And What Does That Little Dot Do?

That little dot that you often see after a note simply makes the note last longer by half its value. If the note is a quarter note (♩), a dot added (♩.) gives it the value of a quarter note and an eighth note (♩ ♪). Look at the eighth notes and dotted quarter notes in the song on page 124. You will see them in measures of 2, 4, 6, and 8.

The combination of these two notes (♪ ♩.) makes up a length of four eighth notes (♪ ♪. ♪ ♪).

More on Syncopation

You learned on page 20 what syncopation is. It's a kind of shifting of emphasis of the beat. Sometimes, musicians will speak of syncopation as "playing on the offbeat." Listen to this American rag "classic." You may have heard it featured in the movie *The Sting*. The composer, Scott Joplin, whose life and work came at the turn of the twentieth century, has been the subject of renewed interest in the last few years. Listen for the syncopation—the off beats—especially the ones that look like this: ♪ ♩ ♪

 The Entertainer ....Joplin

Here's another, by a pianist and composer who was well known in the nineteenth century. Notice how he uses the same syncopated pattern. Is there any difference in the feeling?

 Pasquinade, "Caprice"......................Gottschalk

It's fun to take some "square rhythm" songs and "jazz them up" with syncopation. Try singing this jazz version of *Row, Row, Row Your Boat*.

 Row, Row, Row Your Boat (jazz version)

Playing Along

Now that you know something about rhythm, learn to sing this song, and then add rhythm accompaniment to it.

I'm an Old Cowhand

Words and Music by Johnny Mercer

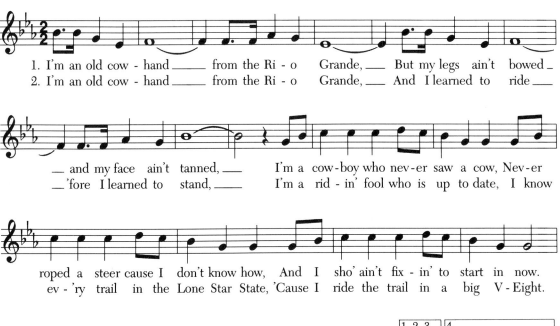

3. I'm an old cowhand
    From the Rio Grande,
    And I come to town
    Just to hear the band,
    I know all the songs that the cowboys know,
    'Bout the big corral where the dogies go,
    'Cause I learned them all on the radio.
    Yippy-I-O-Ki-Ay . . .

4. I'm an old cowhand
    From the Rio Grande,
    Where the West is wild,
    Round the Borderland,
    Where the buffalo roam around the zoo,
    And the good folks make you a rug or two,
    And the old Bar X is a Bar-B-Q.
    Yippy-I-O-Ki-Ay . . .

And now add some or all of these rhythm parts. If you don't have the instruments called for here, use any substitute.

Tempo

Have you ever noticed that the music you sing or play is never the same speed? Sometimes it's slow, sometimes fast. Sometimes it's right in between. The speed of a piece of music, whether slow or fast, is called *tempo*. Often, composers will try to tell performers how fast or slow to perform their music. They will sometimes use Italian words. Here are some of the terms composers might use.

Presto—very fast

Allegro—lively

Moderato—moderate

Andante—walking tempo

Adagio—slow

Largo—very slow

Which of those words might you choose to describe the pictures above?

The problem with the Italian words on page 128 is that they mean different things to different people. Your interpretation of "very fast" may be quite different from that of your classmate's, whose "very fast" may not be nearly as fast as yours. This is why a piece of music may be performed in so many different ways; the performer must bring his or her own sense of tempo to it.

Some composers have tried to be more precise about the tempos they want. They often use a machine called a *metronome*. It establishes an unwavering beat at just the tempo the composer wants. The metronome is very old; it was first used extensively by Beethoven. Unfortunately, music is not a precise art, and the metronome, while useful, has not answered the question, What is the perfect tempo?

Tempo can also change within a space of time. This can often be clearly heard in spoken dialogue. Listen to this brief exchange from an imaginary radio show. You can hear the speeding up and slowing down of the dialogue.

 "Sherlock Holmes" Scene

Composers sometimes exploit the concept of getting faster and getting slower just for its own sake. Listen to this well-known composition by Brazilian composer Heitor Villa-Lobos (HAY tohr   veel lah LOH bohsh). His musical description of a train getting faster (*accelerando*) and slowing down (*ritardando*) has become a favorite of concertgoers all over the world.

 The Little Train of the Caipira . . . . Villa-Lobos

Harmony—Getting It All Together

Do you remember the harmony from the Middle Ages? You read about it on page 73 and listened to an example of it. Basically it was a melody duplicated, or doubled, at another interval, usually the fifth or the fourth interval below the melody. In this example of "Row, Row, Row Your Boat," the melody is harmonized at the fourth below. (The example is in the key of G to keep it on the staff.)

Row, row, row your boat, gent-ly down the stream, _

Mer-ri-ly, mer-ri-ly, mer-ri-ly, mer-ri-ly, Life is but a dream. _

While doubling of melodies began with the intervals of the fourth and fifth, the third and the sixth eventually prevailed as the intervals of choice. In some countries, such as Mexico, the use of the third as a harmonizing interval is almost a national musical characteristic. Learn to sing this song from Mexico and work out the harmonization in thirds. When you have learned it, try doubling the melody a fourth below. How does the feeling of the song change?

De colores

Mexican Folk Song   English Words by Alice Firgau and Samuele Maquí

1. De ___ co - lo - res, ___ De co - lo - res se vis - ten los cam - pos en
deh   koh - loh - rehs   deh koh - loh - rehs seh vees-tehn lohs cahm-pohs ehn
When ___ the mead-ows, ___ when the mead-ows burst forth in the cool dew - y

la pri - ma - ve - ra, _____ De ___ co -
lah pree - mah - veh - rah   deh   koh -
col - ors of spring-time; _____ When ___ the

lo - res, ___ De co - lo - res son los pa - ja - ri - tos que vie - nen dea
loh - rehs   deh koh - loh - rehs sohn lohs pah-hah - ree-tohs keh vee-eh-nehn deh ah
swal - lows, ___ when the swal-lows come wing-ing in clouds of bright col - ors from

fue - ra, _____ De _____ co - lo - res, _____
fooeh - rah deh koh - loh - rehs
far off; _____ *When _____ the rain - bow,* __

_ De co - lo - res es el ar - co i - res que ve - mos lu - cir, _____
deh koh - loh - rehs ehs ehl ahr - coh ee - rehs keh veh-mohs loo - seer
_ when the rain-bow spreads rib-bons of col - or all o - ver the sky, _____

Y por e - so los gran - des a - mo - res de mu - chos co - lo - res me
ee pohr ay - soh lohs grahn-dehs ah - moh-rehs deh moo-chohs koh - loh - rehs meh
Then I know why the splen-dors of true love are great and their col - ors, the

1. gus - tan a mi. _____ **2.** gus - tan a mi. _____
goos - tahn ah mee goos - tahn ah mee
best ones of all. _____ *best ones of all.* _____

De Colores, traditional, arranged, and adapted by Joan Baez © 1974, Chandos Music. (ASCAP)

2. Canta el gallo, Canta el gallo con el   kahn-tah ehl gah-yoh kahn-tah ehl gah-yo kawn ehl
    quiri quiri quiri quiri quiri;   kee-ree kee-ree kee-ree kee-ree kee-ree
    La gallina, La gallina con el   lah gah-yee-na lah gah-yee-na kawn ehl
    cara cara cara cara cara;   kah-rah kah-rah kah-rah kah-rah kah-rah
    Los polluelos, Los polluelos con el   lohs poh-yweh-lohs lohs poh-yweh-lohs kawn ehl
    pio pio pio pio pi,   pee-oh pee-oh pee-oh pee-oh pee
    Y por eso los grandes amores de muchos   ee paw ray-soh lohs gran-dehs ah-mo-rehs deh moo-chohs
    colores me gustan a mi. *(2 times)*   koh-loh-rehs meh goos-tahn ah mee *(2 times)*

> *Hear the rooster, Hear the rooster that calls*
>   *quiri quiri quiri quiri quiri,*
> *Hear his lady, Hear his lady sing back*
>   *cara cara cara cara cara,*
> *Hear the small ones, Hear the small ones call out*
>   *pio pio pio pio pi,*
> *And my favorite folks are the folks who wear colors,*
>   *the colors so pleasant to me. (2 times)*

Harmony, Harmony, Quite Contrary

Harmonizing a melody does not always mean moving in parallel motion. Sometimes, harmony parts may also move in an opposite direction from that of the melody line. This kind of contrary motion can provide more variety in a piece. Here is a song you may have sung many times at camp. Listen for the way the countermelody works as a mirror image of the melody at the beginning of the first three phrases.

Tell Me Why

Countermelody (2nd time only)   Traditional

2. Be - cause God made ___ the stars to shine,

1. Tell ___ me why ___ the stars do shine,
2. Be - cause God made ___ the stars to shine,

Be - cause God made ___ the i - vy twine,

Tell ___ me why ___ the i - vy twines, Then
Be - cause God made ___ the i - vy twine,

Be - cause God made ___ the sky so blue,

tell ___ me why ___ the sky is blue,
Be - cause God made ___ the sky so blue,

Be - cause God made you so sweet ___ and true.

And I will tell you why I ___ love you.
Be - cause God made you so sweet ___ and true.

Polyphonic Texture

On page 73 you learned what polyphonic texture is. It is two or more voices singing independent vocal lines. A canon, or a round, can be a good example of polyphonic texture. (But be careful. Some rounds are really homophonic—all voices singing different notes but moving in the same rhythm.) This round is a good representation of the polyphonic round. If you examine each line, you will see that each one is different in melodic direction and rhythm.

A Home on the Rolling Sea

Words and Music by David Eddleman

I Give me a home on the roll - ing sea, and let me be a sail - or;

II Let me a sail - or be;

III Let me sail off on a ship for a life on the rol - lick - ing sea.

The Fugue—A Flighty Form that Always Has an Answer

While the round may be the simplest imitative form, the fugue (FYOOG), from the Italian word *fuga*, meaning "flight," can be the most complex. The fugue begins like a canon, but it adds other lines and parts, including some sections that may be only bits and pieces of what has gone before. Often the fugue will end with a stretto (STREHT toh), in which the subject—the melody—enters rapidly, overlapping the other voices very quickly.

Listen to this fugue by J.S. Bach. Can you hear the subject entering and reentering? When you have heard it, you may want to play the short fugue on page 134. It contains all the parts of a fugue. Try playing it on recorders with your classmates.

Fugue in D Minor . . . . Bach

133

Fugue in G

David Eddleman

Tie the Music Up with Chords

Triads, the most common chords, come from the scale that the melody is based on. A triad can be built on any scale tone just by adding thirds, like these triads in G major.

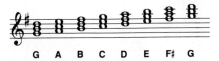

G A B C D E F♯ G

For "Ode to Joy" you will need three chords—the G-major (G, B, and D), D-major (D, F♯, and A), and A-major (A, C♯, and E). Play even quarter notes on piano or bells changing chords with the chord symbol over the music.

Ode to Joy

Music by Ludwig van Beethoven   English Words by Henry Van Dyke   Arranged by Alan Seale

Henry van Dyke, "Hymn of Joy" from the Poems of Henry van Dyke. Reprinted with the permission of Charles Scribner's Sons.

Tone Color—The Sounds of Music

Noise

I like noise.
The wh*oo*p of a boy, the thu*d* of a hoof,
The ra*tt*le of rain on a galvanized roof,
The hu*bb*ub of traffic, the r*oar* of a train,
The *throb* of machinery n*um*bing the brain,
The *switch*ing of wires in an overhead tram.
The ru*sh* of the wind, a door on the slam.
The boom of the thunder, the *crash* of the wave,
The din of a river that *races* and *raves*,
The *crack* of a rifle, the *clank* of a pail,
The strident tattoo of a *swift-slapp*ing sail.
From any old sound that the silen*ce* destroys
Arises a gamut of soul-stirring joys.
I like noise.

J. Pope
© PUNCH London

6 *Collage of Sounds*

The collage of sounds you heard was a mixture of the sounds
produced by objects all around. Could you tell them apart? If you
could tell what the sounds were, you were identifying their *tone
color*—the way they sound. The rain has a "rain color," the car
horn has a "car horn color," the truck horn has a "truck horn
color," and so on.

Composers use tone color to add to the expression of their music just as painters use the colors of the spectrum to create and enhance feeling in their paintings. Look at the reproduction of Vincent Van Gogh's famous painting *The Starry Night*. It is a night scene, yet there is a torrent of color—oranges, blues, yellows, even whites. The swirls of color around the haloed stars are reflected in the swirls of blue and purple in the hills in the background. The feeling is that of motion within stillness, power within calm. Could Van Gogh have achieved these feelings and effects in any other way or with other colors? It makes no difference, really. The work stands as a piece unique in itself, forming its own character from the painter's colors and shapes.

The Starry Night
Vincent van Gogh

Sing Those Golden Tones

Voices, too, vary widely in their sound and quality. Barbra Streisand's voice does not have the same tone color as Lena Horne's, and both voices are quite unlike Patti LaBelle's. Plácido Domingo's voice is big and brilliant and filled with the kind of grand-opera tone quality we would expect. Louis Armstrong's distinctive "laryngitis" sound is immediately recognizable to almost everyone. With singers, individual tone color is part of their trademark. When someone hears a new recording by one of these artists, it is important to the singer that he or she be recognizable, even though no announcement has been made about the performer's identity.

Listen to two vocalists perform "Send In the Clowns" from *A Little Night Music*. Can you hear how the quality and color of each voice changes the expression of the song?

 "Send In the Clowns" (Judy Collins) . . . . Sondheim

 "Send In the Clowns" (Lisa Skiba) . . . . Sondheim

Three Performers, One Piece

Even the same instrumental piece can sound different in the hands of different performers. Listen to these three performances of Chopin's *Waltz in C♯ Minor*. What differences can you hear in them?

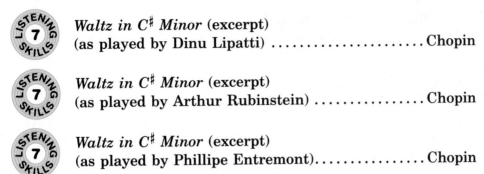

Waltz in C♯ Minor (excerpt)
(as played by Dinu Lipatti) . . . . Chopin

Waltz in C♯ Minor (excerpt)
(as played by Arthur Rubinstein) . . . . Chopin

Waltz in C♯ Minor (excerpt)
(as played by Phillipe Entremont). . . . . Chopin

Some Singers Do It All

Today there is a singer who is combining the career of a rock singer with that of an opera singer. Listen to two recordings of Peter Hofmann, a young German tenor, as he shows off his ability to be both "popular" and "serious."

Die Walküre, "Winterstürme" . . . . Wagner

The Long and Winding Road . . . . Lennon and McCartney

Instrumental Music's Four Basic Colors

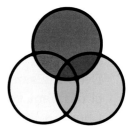

You know that the color spectrum consists of three primary colors—red, yellow, and blue. All other colors are made by combining these three colors in many different ways.

Music, as we have seen, has color, too. In addition to the various vocal colors, instruments fall into four basic color categories. Look at these pictures and listen to some music specially written for each group.

The Brass

LISTENING SKILLS **7**

Brass Quartet "In Honorem Paul Hindemith," Movement 1 .... Eddleman

The Woodwinds

LISTENING SKILLS **7**

La cheminée du Roi René, Movement 1 .... Milhaud

The Strings

LISTENING SKILLS **7**

Adagio for Strings .... Barber

The Percussion

LISTENING SKILLS **8**

The Aztec Gods, Movement 1 .... Read

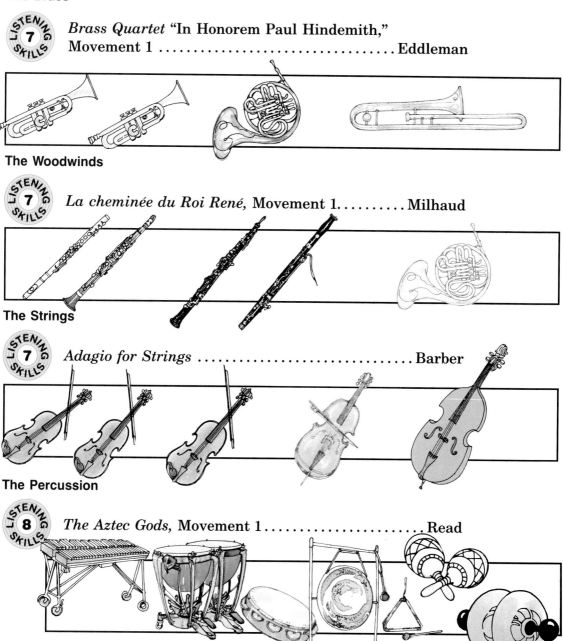

How's Your Color Sense?

Composers, when they write for instruments, usually have a particular set of instruments in mind for their compositions. *Tales from the Latin Woods* is just such a piece. The composer had a very specific set of tone colors in mind for this piece, and each part can be most easily played by the instrument for which he wrote it.

Listen to *Tales from the Latin Woods* as played by each of the four instrumental groups. Then decide which group sounds most appropriate. Don't worry if you guess wrong! Music is an art, not a science, and you may very well hear the brass, woodwinds, strings, or percussion as more appropriate than the composer's solution. The composer won't mind!

 Tales from the Latin Woods . . . . Eddleman
1. **Brass group**
2. **String group**
3. **Woodwind group**
4. **Percussion group**

Listen to the way one composer put all the instrumental colors together in "Russian Sailors' Dance." The Call Chart will help you recognize the instruments.

Call Chart 7

 The Red Poppy, "Russian Sailors' Dance" . . . . Glière

1. **Introduction—full orchestra; *ff*; fast**
2. **Low strings, low brass; *f*, then *mf*; slow**
3. **Clarinet, strings, tambourine; *mp*; slow.**
4. **Clarinet and piccolo solos, strings accompany; *mf*; slow.**
5. **Horns, woodwinds, tambourine; *f*; fast**
6. **Strings, tambourine, brass; *ff*; slow**
7. **Oboe, clarinet, low strings pizzicato (plucked); *mp*; slow**
8. **Woodwinds, strings, brass, percussion; *ff*; very fast**
9. **Full orchestra, brass section predominates; *ff*; fast**
10. **Full orchestra to end; bass drum "stinger"**

Patterns in Sound

Sounds have patterns. Listen to this group of sounds from the world you live in.

Collage of Environmental Sounds

There are patterns in music, as well. All your favorite songs are built on different melody and rhythm patterns that repeat in different ways. They help to make the song sound "logical," as if it all belongs together. This song has a number of patterns. Can you find them?

Scatterbox

Words and Music by Steven L. Rosenhaus

Cool, moderate swing

1. I don't need words to sing a song; I can go on all day.
2. Make it all up as you go a-long; you don't e-ven need to rhyme

And if you want you can sing a-long, Just lis-ten to me and re-peat what I say:
And if it swings you can say that you are hav-ing a mar-ve-lous, won-der-ful time!

142

143

Team Up with Your Pattern

Can you make rhythm patterns out of your name and your friends' names? *David,* for example, becomes ♩ ♩ ♩ ♩
Da - vid, Da - vid

and *Carolyn* would be [rhythm notation]. Try making up rhythm
Car-o-lyn, Car-o-lyn,

patterns with your classmates' names and chant them together.

Here is a chant ensemble based on the names of well-known football teams. First clap the patterns, then chant the names.

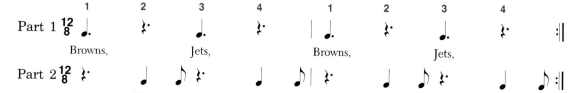

Part 1 — Browns, Jets, Browns, Jets,

Part 2 — Tam - pa, Dal - las, Tam - pa, Dal - las,

Part 3 — Rams, Los An-ge-les Rams, Los An-ge-les

Part 4 — New Jer - sey Gi-ants, New Jer - sey Gi-ants,

Part 5 — In-di-an - a-po-lis Colts, In-di-an - a-po-lis Colts,

Now try chanting the "football team pattern" with this recording.

Dooji-Wooji .... Ellington

144

A Layer Cake of Patterns

Have you ever heard a Latin American instrumental group playing *salsa*? *Salsa* is a Spanish word meaning "sauce" and in this case, it's *hot* sauce. The excitement you may feel when hearing salsa or any other Latin style is often created by the layering of melody and rhythm patterns that repeat over and over, usually with an improvised instrumental or vocal solo on top. Do you remember the African rhythm complex on page 10?

Look at the melodic-rhythmic ostinato pattern at the bottom of this layer cake. Learn to sing the ostinato, then sing it with the recording.

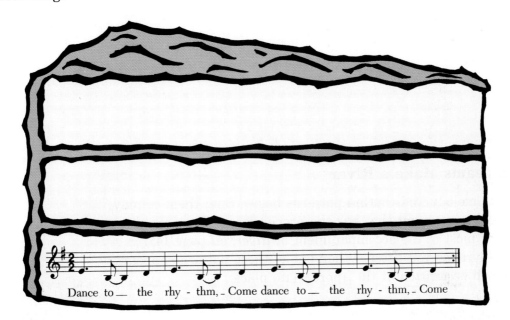

Dance to — the rhy - thm, — Come dance to — the rhy - thm, — Come

Do the Mambo . . . . Eisman and Carr

Composers have used ostinatos for centuries as a way to hold a piece together. Often they weave many variations above and around the ostinato. Listen to this piece to hear how the composer does just that. The ostinato looks like this.

Play it on the piano or on a bass-clef instrument. Then listen to it with the variations.

The Bells of St. Geneviève (excerpt) . . . . Marais

145

A Composer's Best Friend Is His Pattern

Composers who use electronic instruments to create their works often use the same devices as do composers who use *acoustical* (ah KOO stih kl) means—natural sound. Ostinato, for example, is still a favorite device of the electronic composer, as it is with the acoustical composer. Edward Smaldone has created a short piece for synthesizer using many different patterns. Try to hear how he organizes those patterns.

 Piece for Synthesizer . . . . Smaldone

Little Streams Make a River

Look at the melody and rhythm patterns below. Sing them or play them on any instrument that has the proper range. They are the patterns for most of the accompaniment of *River,* on page 147. Follow the lyric as you listen. When one of these patterns appears, its letter will be written at the appropriate place.

River ⑧

Eugene McDaniels

Introduction: A and B

A and B	There's a river somewhere, Flows through the lives of everyone; And it flows through the valleys and the mountains and the meadows of time.
	There's a star in the sky, Brightenin' the lives of everyone; I know it brightens the valleys and the mountains and the meadows of time. Yes, it do.
Free improvisation	*Chorus*: Yes, it do. There's a voice from the past
A and C	Speaks through the lives of everyone; I know it speaks through the valleys and the mountains
A and C	and the meadows of time.
	There's a smile in your eye
A and C	Brightens the lives of everyone; I know it brightens the valleys and the mountains
A and C	and the meadows of time. Yes, it do.
Free improvisation with A and C	*Chorus*: Yes, it do.
	There's a short song of love
C and D	Sings through the lives of everyone; And it sings through the valleys and the mountains
C and D	and the meadows of time.
	There's a sweet song of love
C	That sings through the lives of everyone; I know it sings through the valleys and the mountains
C	and the meadows of time.
Free improvisation	Yes, it do.
	Chorus: Yes, it do.
	There's a river somewhere,
D	Flows through the lives of everyone; I know it flows through the valleys and the mountains
C and D	and the meadows of time.
	There's a sweet song of love
C	Sweetenin' the lives of everyone; And it sweetens the valleys and the mountains
C	and the meadows of time.
Free improvisation	Yes, it do.
	Chorus: Yes, it do.

Patterns for Playing

This Old Hammer 🎱

Black American Work Song

1. This old ham-mer _____ killed John Hen-ry, _____ This old
2. Take this ham-mer _____ to the walk-in' boss, _____ Take this

ham-mer _____ killed John Hen-ry, _____ This old ham-mer _____
ham-mer _____ to the walk-in' boss, _____ Take this ham-mer _____

_____ killed John Hen-ry, _____ but it won't kill me, _____
_____ to the walk-in' boss, _____ Tell_ him I'm gone, _____

_____ no, it won't_ kill me. _____
_____ Oh, _____ tell him I'm gone. _____

Try accompanying "This Old Hammer" using bells. First line up the bells like this.

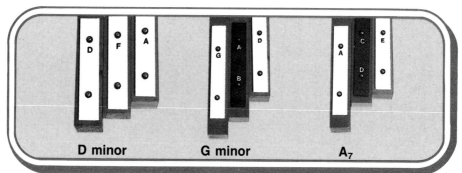

Here is the chord pattern: D min. | A₇ | D min. | D min. | G min. | A₇ |
D min. | D min. | Try playing the chord pattern on bells, using equal
quarter notes in each measure: ♩ ♩ ♩ ♩. Then try a more complicated
rhythm, such as ♪♩ ♪♩ ♩ or ♩ ♫ ♫ ♩. (Do you remember the
name for that one?—it's syncopation!), or perhaps ♩ ♫♫ ♫ ♩.
There are numerous combinations you can try. Write your rhythm
patterns on the board. When you have enough of them, try layering
them as in *River* or the African rhythm complex. The layering can get
as intricate as you like, but remember, the secret is—*be musical.*

How's That Again?

Some composers have constructed whole pieces from the simplest of ideas—ideas that repeat over and over with changes of key, orchestration, or dynamic level. The Norwegian composer Edvard Grieg (GREEG) wrote a piece for orchestra called *In the Hall of the Mountain King.* The basic rhythm of the theme is

and the basic melodic idea is

As you listen, you will hear almost no change in the rhythm, and the melody is constantly repeated.

  Peer Gynt, "In the Hall of the Mountain King" . . . . . Grieg

Edvard Grieg
(1843–1907)

Grieg is so closely associated with the land and legends of Norway that few people realize his ancestry was Scottish. His grandfather (who spelled the name "Gre*ig*") had emigrated to Norway from Scotland around 1765.

Grieg was a *nationalist* composer, a composer whose national background was constantly reflected in his compositions. Nationalism, which was an important movement during the Romantic period, depended a great deal on folk music, as well as on music written to *sound* like folk music. Grieg chose to write his music so that it would capture the flavor of Norwegian folk music. His lyric melodies caused many people to call him the Chopin of the North.

3+2+2=7

On page 116 you began a study of meters. You learned about beats grouped in units, about those units being in groups of two, three, and four. And you even found that meter in 2 and meter in 3 could be combined in unusual ways, as in "Tumbalalaika," on page 120. Go back and look at the last section of "Tumbalalaika" where the meter is shown as $\frac{3}{4}$ $\frac{2}{4}$. Now imagine that the bar line between each $\frac{3}{4}$ measure and $\frac{2}{4}$ measure has been removed. How would you now express that larger measure in a meter signature? If you said, "Call it $\frac{5}{4}$," you were right. $\frac{5}{4}$ would be an accurate description of the meter of that last section—five beats per measure, with the quarter note ($\quarternote$) representing the beat. Now listen to this "rap" piece. What do you think its meter is?

⑧ DANCIN'   *Sole to Soul*   **Words by Connie Rybak**

1	2	3	1	2	1	2
GIRLS					*BOYS*	
On	the	street,	Let's	dance,	Let's	dance,
Feel	the	beat,	Great	chance,	Great	chance,
Twist	and	roll	Clock	- wise,	Clock	- wise,
Keep	con	- trol	Rock	- wise,	Rock	- wise.
BOYS					*GIRLS*	
Try	the	stage,	Up,	down,	Up,	down,
It's	the	rage	Down	- town,	Down	- town,
Now	that	glide,	Toe	- heel,	Toe	- heel,
What	a	ride,	Un	- real,	Un	- real.
GIRLS					*BOYS*	
When	I	move	Free	- ly,	Free	- ly,
Trou -	bles	soothed,	See	me,	See	me,
Feel	my	best	Danc	- in',	Danc	- in',
Need	no	rest	Pranc	- in',	Pranc	- in'.
BOYS					*GIRLS*	
Add	more	voice,	Hear	ye,	Hear	ye,
It's	your	choice,	Clear	- ly,	Clear	- ly,
Danc -	in's	role,	Real	- ly,	Real	- ly,
EVERYONE						
Sole	to	soul.	*(stamp,*	*clap*	*stamp,*	*clap)*

© 1988 Connie Rybak

Did you guess that the meter is in 7? The text of *Dancin'* groups its beats into a pattern of **1** 2 3, **1** 2, **1** 2. Why, do you think, are the beats divided this way and not **1** 2, **1** 2, **1** 2 3 or **1** 2, **1** 2 3, **1** 2? (*Hint:* Look at the way the word accents fall.)

Have you ever sung the song, "Oh, Susanna"? If you have you may remember that it is in duple meter—beats grouped in twos. Try singing this contemporary arrangement of Foster's tune. You can see from the meter signature that the meter is in 7. Look at the music. Can you tell just by looking at it which breakdown best fits the music—2 3 2, 3 2 2, or 2 2 3?

Oh, Susanna

Words and Music by Stephen Foster   Arranged by Sol Berkowitz

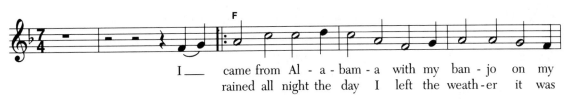

I___ came from Al - a - bam - a with my ban - jo on my
rained all night the day I left the weath - er it was

knee, I'm _ go - in' to Lou' - si - an - a my ___ true love for to see. It __
dry, The _ sun _ so hot I froze to death, Su - san - na don't you

cry. ___ Oh, Su - san - na, ___ Oh, don't you cry for me, For I've

come from Al - a - bam - a with my ban - jo on my knee, For I've come from Al - a -

bam - a with a ban - jo on my knee. _____

More Beats Again—Meter in 10

Can you count the meter of this piece? Believe it or not, it's a meter in 10! Follow the score as you listen to an excerpt from Leonard Bernstein's *Chichester Psalms*. Bernstein, a well-known American composer and former conductor of the New York Philharmonic, suggests that the meter in 10 be broken down this way: 1 2, 1 2 3, 1 2, 1 2 3—really a kind of counting in two groups of five!

This excerpt, based on the original Hebrew text of Psalm 131, begins in the middle of the measure with the words *Adonai, Adonai*. The beat will be

6 7 8 9 10 1 2 3 4 5 6 7 8 9 10 1 2 3 4 5

A - do - nai, A - do - nai,_____ Lo ga - vah__ li - bi,_____

Now it's up to you. Can you count the beats in the rest of the piece? Don't worry if you get lost. One of Bernstein's reasons for using this unusual meter may have been to obscure the beat grouping so that the listener *wouldn't* know what meter it was in. He may have wanted a feeling of no clear beat grouping at all, and meter in 10 certainly helps to accomplish that goal!

 Chichester Psalms (excerpt) .... Bernstein

Beats Within Beats (or 6, 3, or 2?)

Why is a football field divided into five-yard lengths? Why not one-yard lengths or even one-*foot* lengths? Can you imagine what that football field would look like with one-foot divisions? Probably like a picket fence! Obviously, such small divisions would confuse the eye of the football fan sitting high up in the bleachers.

Sometimes the tempo of a piece of music is so fast that individual beats, like individual feet and yards, go by too quickly to be counted comfortably and without confusion. If you play any piece at all you can probably play "Chopsticks." Here it is in two different settings. One is slow, the other faster. Can you see any difference in the meter?

Try conducting. You learned how to conduct meter in 2 on page 116. Of course, now you're faced with a meter in 6, and you haven't learned how to conduct in six yet. To compound this, try conducting in two, three eighth notes to a beat, and see how it works. You see, like the football field that gathers up smaller units and lays them out in larger, easier-to-handle bunches, $\frac{6}{8}$ meter turns small groups of six beats into two large beats of three smaller notes. To compound this situation further, it's almost as if you were conducting in two, with every beat having a triplet! And to compound it even more, this kind of "meter-in-a-meter" is called *compound meter*. When you were younger, you might have seen this signature written as $\frac{2}{}$—a good clue to how it feels and works.

Three as One

This song has a meter signature of $\frac{3}{8}$. Do you remember what that means? It means that there are three beats in each measure, and the eighth note (♪) represents one beat. But listen to the song once before you decide what the meter really is. How does it feel when you *sing* it?

Con el vito

Folk Song from Spain   Arranged by Darrell Peter   English Version by Aura Kontra

Con el vi - to, vi - to, vi - to,___ Con el
kohn ehl vee - toh vee - toh vee - toh kohn ehl

vi - to, vi - to, va.___ Con el vi - to, vi - to,
vee - toh vee - toh vah kohn ehl vee - toh vee - toh

vi - to,___ Con el vi - to, vi - to, va.___ To the
vee - toh kohn ehl vee - toh vee - toh vah *U - na*
oo - nah

bull - fights in Se - vi - lla, Went the Span - ish la - dy
ma - la - gue - ña fue a Se - vi - lla a ver los
mah - lah - ghen - nyah fweh ah seh - vee - yah ah vehr lohs

rid - ing; She was cap - tured on the high - way
to - ros; Y en la mi - tad del ca - mi - no
toh - rohs yehn lah mee - tahd dehl cah - mee - noh

D.C. al Fine

By some Moor - ish ban - dits hid - ing.
La cau - ti - va - ron los mo - ros.
lah kow - tee - vah - rohn lohs moh - rohs.

154

It goes like the wind, doesn't it? It would be impossible to conduct "Con el vito" in three. But if you understand that the beat is actually *one beat per measure* rather than three per measure as the signature would show, then it is easy. Try conducting just *downbeats*—one per measure—1|1|1|1|1|1| and so on. You'll find that it works well. In some ways, just as $\frac{6}{8}$ can be rethought as $\frac{2}{}$, so the $\frac{3}{8}$ of "Con el vito" can be rethought as $\frac{1}{}$.

Another Subdivision on the Musical Landscape

On the chart on page 123, you discovered that notes could be divided evenly into other notes, a quarter (♩) into two eighths (♫) or a half (♩) into two quarters (♩ ♩), for example. Composers, especially those who have been influenced by African rhythms, sometimes play little "accent games" with these subdivisions. Look at these quarter notes and their subdivided eighth notes.

Can you tell what has happened to the bottom line of eighth notes? Instead of the accents falling on the first of each two eighths (♫ ♫ ♫) as in the middle line, the accents are falling on the first of each *three* eighths (♫ ♫ ♫). It's almost as if a $\frac{6}{8}$ meter is being thrown against a $\frac{3}{4}$ meter. Listen to a group of percussionists playing the above pattern of cross-rhythms, then try it yourself.

 *Cross-rhythms*

Now try playing the cross-rhythms yourself with the Zulu folk song *Mangwani Mpulele.*

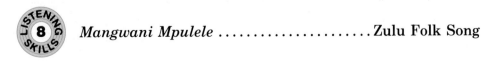 *Mangwani Mpulele* . . . . Zulu Folk Song

An "Unsquare" Dance

While you may like the outfits in the left or middle pictures, many people might feel that the picture on the right shows a man who has dressed with taste. In the left picture he is wearing far too many colors. In the middle picture he is monochromatic—too much of one color. At the right he seems nicely coordinated.

Music also must have balance. There must be similar elements with a number of contrasting elements as well. Look at these melodies. Which has too much repetition? Too little repetition? Which is just right?

Dave Brubeck was looking for a way to both unify and give variety to this piece. As you listen, you may learn that it is in a meter of 7. (That's why it's called "unsquare.") Does the metric feeling have anything to do with its unity or variety?

Unsquare Dance . . . . Brubeck

Here is the meter scheme for *Unsquare Dance*. Try playing it on percussion instruments.

Meter	1	2	3	4	5	6	7
High instrument	x		x		x	x	
Low instrument	x			x		x	

You probably realized that it is the metric feel—acting as an ostinato throughout the piece—that acts as a unifier. The variations that Brubeck weaves over the ostinato provide variety and interest to this piece that is considered by many to be a twentieth-century jazz classic.

Diagramming Meter

Unsquare Dance

1	2	3	4	5	6	7

Bass | A | x | G | x : A | x | x
notes | A | x | G | x : A | x | x
| D | x | C | x : D | x | x
| A | x | G | x : A | x | x
| E | x | D | x : E | x | x
| A | x | G | x : A | x | x

Rock Around the Clock

1	2	3	4	1	2	3	4

Chords | D | D
| D | D_7
| G_7 | G_7
| D | D
| A_7 | G_7
| D | D

The letters in the diagram for *Unsquare Dance* are the notes the string bass plays. The x's are the hand claps heard throughout the piece. For "Rock Around the Clock," the diagram shows a pattern of chords that repeats throughout the song, beginning with the first verse. These bass notes, hand claps, and chord patterns help to give the pieces a unity—a "glue" that holds them together.

Set your bells up to play the triads with "Rock Around the Clock."

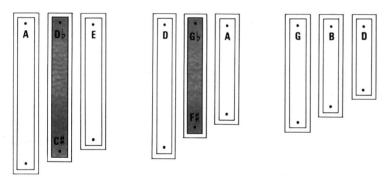

Rock Around the Clock ⑨

Words and Music by M. Freedman and J. Deknight

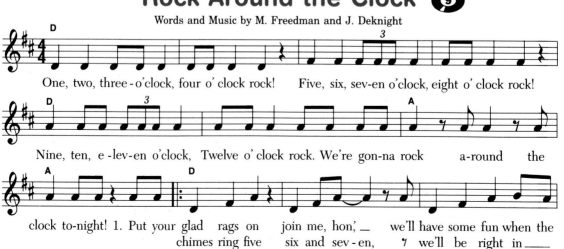

One, two, three - o'clock, four o' clock rock!   Five, six, sev-en o'clock, eight o' clock rock!

Nine, ten, e -lev-en o'clock, Twelve o' clock rock. We're gon-na rock   a-round   the

clock to-night! 1. Put your glad   rags on   join me, hon',__   we'll have some fun when the
                 chimes ring five   six and sev-en,   we'll be right in____

clock strikes one, We're gon-na rock a - round the clock to - night, _ we're gon-na
sev - enth heav'n, We're gon-na rock a - round the clock to - night, _ we're gon-na

rock, rock, rock 'til the broad day-light, _ We're gon-na rock, we're gon-na rock _ a - round _
rock, rock, rock 'til the broad day-light, _ We're gon-na rock, we're gon-na rock _ a - round _

_ the clock _ to night. _____ 2. When the clock strikes two,
_ the clock _ to night. _____ 4. When it's eight, nine, ten, e -

three and four, if the band slows down we'll yell for more, We're gon-na rock a - round the
lev - en, too, I'll be go - in' strong and so will you, We're gon-na rock a - round the

clock to - night, _ we're gon-na rock, rock, rock 'til the broad day-light, _ We're gon-na
clock to - night, _ we're gon-na rock, rock, rock 'til the broad day-light, _ We're gon-na

rock, we're gon-na rock _ a - round ___ the clock _ to-night. ___ 3. When the
rock, we're gon-na rock _ a - round ___ the clock _ to-night. ___

5. When the clock strikes twelve, we'll cool off. Then _ start-a

rock - in' 'round the clock a - gain, _ We're gon-na rock a - round the

clock to - night, _ we're gon-na rock, rock, rock, 'til the broad day-light, _ We're gon-na

rock, we're gon-na rock _ a - round ___ the clock _ to - night. ___

159

Bluesin' on the Bottom, Rockin' on the Top

Joe Turner Blues . . . . Traditional

You have heard a 12-bar blues. Both *Unsquare Dance* (in its divided-measure version) and "Rock Around the Clock" are loosely based on a chord progression used in the 12-bar blues. That is a three-phrase pattern of twelve measures with the chord progression:

I   I   I   I₇   IV₇ IV₇ I   I   V₇ IV₇ I   I

"It's Not So Easy Being Me" is based on the blues pattern in Eᵇ major. To build a harmonic accompaniment in the key of Eᵇ, you will need I, IV, and V chords in that key. To make the chords even "bluesier," add a *seventh* on top of the chords.

It's Not So Easy Bein' Me

Words and Music by Lawrence Eisman

1. I don't see __ why there must be __ so man-y do's and don'ts in our so-
   know that I __ am not the best __ at an-y-thing I do, I fall be-
3. I don't see __ why I must be __ so caught up in a race for pop-u-

ci-e-ty, __ Which seem de-signed __ with me in mind __ as
hind the rest, __ It's not that I __ don't care or try, __ it's
lar-i-ty, __ To live my life __ through oth-er's eyes __ when

if I did-n't know how to act re-fined. __ If you'd look __ I'm
e-ven got me fooled 'cause I won-der why, __ It would help __ if
I'm the on-ly one I must sat-is-fy, __ I'd feel re-lieved __ if

sure you'd see __ It's not so eas-y be-in' me. __ 2. I
you would see __ It's not so eas-y be-in' me. __
you'd be-lieve, __ It's not so eas-y be-in' me. __

160

A Rock Progression We Have Known and Loved—I VI IV V₇

If you can play "Chopsticks" on the piano, you can probably play
"Heart and Soul" as well. (It's usually done as a duet with a friend.)
The chord progression is I VI IV V₇ in the key of C. Play these
chords on bells or piano to go with "Those Magic Changes."

Those Magic Changes

from the Broadway musical *Grease*

Words and Music by Warren Casey and Jim Jacobs

161

The Firebird—A Flight of Patterns

Igor Stravinsky's colorful ballet tells the story of an old Russian folk tale. Prince Ivan, lost in a forest, finds a marvelous bird with flaming red feathers. He captures her but then, seeing that she is frightened, releases her. In gratitude the firebird gives the prince one of her feathers to protect him against evil, and she pledges her help should he ever be in trouble. Ivan meets a princess who with her twelve sisters is held prisoner by the evil King Katschei, (КАНТ shay). Katschei tries to cast a spell on Ivan, but Ivan overcomes the wicked sorcerer with his firebird feather. The firebird appears and, placing Katschei in a trance, tells Ivan that Katschei's power lies in a monstrous egg, which she reveals to Ivan. The egg is broken, Katschei perishes, the princess and all of Katschei's prisoners are freed. Ivan and his princess are married in a sumptuous finale. The finale begins with a simple melodic phrase played slowly and quietly.

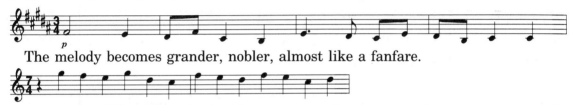

The melody becomes grander, nobler, almost like a fanfare.

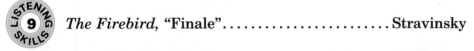

Listen to the way Stravinsky builds textures and uses tone colors to create a satisfying ending to his ballet.

LISTENING SKILLS 9 *The Firebird,* "Finale"........................ Stravinsky

Careers in Music—Composing

Although still a young composer, Suzanne Ciani has been composing for a good many years and has written a substantial body of work. Listen to Ciani as she discusses her life and work. Then listen to her *Composition for Synthesizer*. How does the composer alter the melody pattern? Do you hear a form?

 Careers in Music—Suzanne Ciani

 Composition for Synthesizer ....Ciani

In Unity There Is Strength

Clap this rhythm.

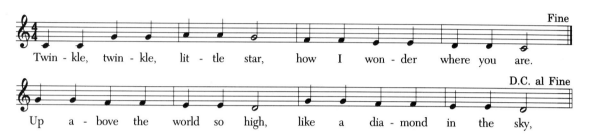

Do you recognize that rhythm? If you said it's the rhythm of "Twinkle, Twinkle, Little Star," you were right. And the rhythm repeats and repeats exactly the same way for the entire song!

Twin - kle, twin - kle, lit - tle star, how I won - der where you are.

Up a - bove the world so high, like a dia - mond in the sky,

The repetition of the same two-measure rhythm pattern has a lot to do with making the song feel unified—a feeling that it's all one piece.

Try singing this patriotic song. Does your understanding of "Twinkle, Twinkle, Little Star" give you a clue to a unifying element in "America, the Beautiful"?

America, the Beautiful

Words by Katherine Lee Bates   Music by Samuel A. Ward   Countermelody by James W. Rooker

Countermelody (4th verse only)

O beau - ti - ful for pa - triot dream___ That

1. O beau - ti - ful for spa - cious skies, For am - ber waves of grain,   For
2. O beau - ti - ful for pil - grim feet, Whose stern im - pas-sioned stress   A

sees be - yond the years, Thy cit - ies gleam un - dimmed by tears! A -

pur - ple moun - tain maj - es - ties A - bove the fruit - ed plain!   A -
thor - ough - fare for free - dom beat A - cross the wil - der - ness!   A -

166

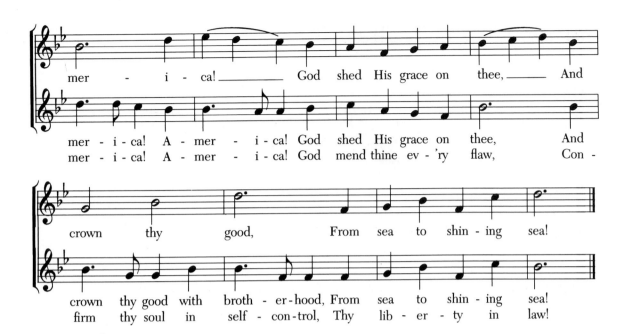

mer - i - ca! _____ God shed His grace on thee, _____ And

mer - i - ca! A - mer - i - ca! God shed His grace on thee, And
mer - i - ca! A - mer - i - ca! God mend thine ev - 'ry flaw, Con -

crown thy good, From sea to shin - ing sea!

crown thy good with broth - er-hood, From sea to shin - ing sea!
firm thy soul in self - con-trol, Thy lib - er - ty in law!

3. O beautiful for heroes proved
   In liberating strife,
   Who more than self their country loved,
   And mercy more than life!
   America! America! May God thy gold refine,
   Till all success be nobleness,
   And ev'ry gain divine!

4. O beautiful for patriot dream
   That sees, beyond the years,
   Thine alabaster cities gleam
   Undimmed by human tears!
   America! America! God shed His grace on thee,
   And crown thy good with brotherhood
   From sea to shining sea!

Even paintings can be based on one basic idea. What about this one? Can you see the single element that unifies the entire canvas?

Jasper Johns. *Three Flags.* 1958. Encaustic on canvas. 30⅞ × 45½ × 5 inches. Collection of Whitney Museum of American Art.

Three Flags
Jasper Johns

Manipulating a Motive

Do you remember what a *motive* is? A motive is a very short musical fragment—usually only a few notes long—that a composer uses to build a piece. Do you remember building "In the Army" from those little parts that preceded it? You were building from phrases there. A motive is even smaller. Look at this one.

Follow the score to see how Sol Berkowitz develops this six-note motive into a full composition for a keyboard instrument.

From Pattern to Piece

You've seen what Berkowitz can do with a motive. Now let's go way back in time, to Johann Sebastian Bach, a composer of the Baroque period who many people think is the greatest composer of all time! Whether he is or isn't, he certainly made motive-building look easy. Look at this motive.

How do you think Bach might have helped his motive grow? Here's the first thing he did

Listen for other ways Bach varied and expanded his motive.

 *Minuet...*Bach

"On My Journey" starts with a distinctive melody and rhythm pattern. How does the rest of the song grow from that pattern?

On My Journey

Black American Traditional Song Arranged by Lawrence Eisman
New Verses by Erik Darling, Lee Hays, Fred Hellerman and Ronnie Gilbert

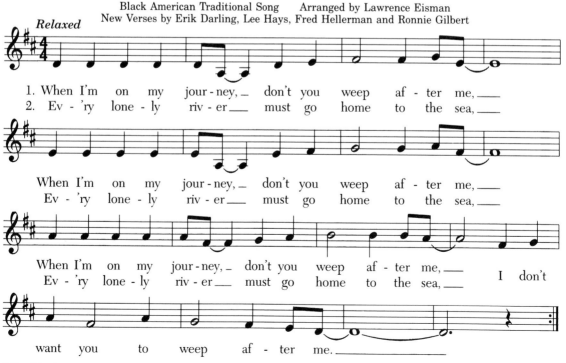

Discern Those Devices! (That Means Recognize Them)

So far we have talked about repetition and inversion (in "Manipulations"), among other compositional devices that composers use. Do you remember discussing sequences on page 111? You will find repetition, inversion, and sequence in each of these songs. In "If I Were You," many measures are empty. How would you fill them, based on the motive in the first two measures?

If I Were You

Words by Connie Rybak   Music by Lawrence Eisman

1. If you were me   and I were you,   no one would know   who was who.
2. If you were me   and I were you,   we'd bet-ter   plan   what we'd do.

We'd look the same   just change our views   ex-ter-nal-ly   give no clues.
I'd be the brains, you'd have the looks,   Har-vard's my choice;   You? No books.

Our fam-i-lies   might get con-fused   if it were you   in my shoes.
Since you're so shy,   and I am not,   think of the deeds   we could plot.

What a great trick   Oh, what a switch,   spirits re-versed,   which is which?
I'd take your place,   get you a date,   just like a worm,   serve as bait.

© 1985 Connie Rybak

By the Waters of Babylon

Words from the Psalms   Music by Philip Hayes (Adapted)

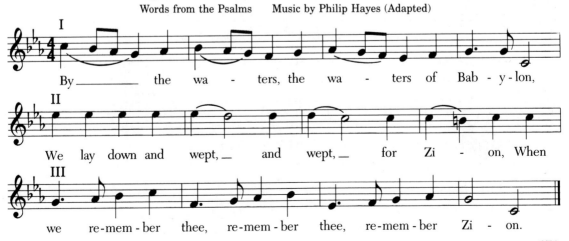

By ____ the wa - ters, the wa - ters of Bab - y - lon,

We lay down and wept, __ and wept, __ for Zi - on, When

we re-mem-ber thee, re-mem-ber thee, re-mem-ber Zi - on.

Filling Out Forms

"That building has an interesting form." "The form of that automobile makes it look like a sports car." "I don't understand this painting. It doesn't seem to have a logical form."

Everything has form. Cars. Trains. Bikes. Even you. We recognize things by their form. Form is a combination of things that are alike and things that are different. In music, form is created by putting like and unlike sections together. "In the Army" had two contrasting sections, one labeled *A*, the other labeled *B*. Do you remember what you did at the end of section B? The *D.S. al Fine* told you to go back to the beginning of section A and sing to the *Fine* (an Italian word that means "end"). When you did that you had a form that could be labeled *ABA*.

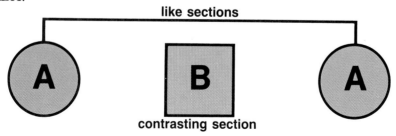

The ABA form became so common to song writers that it has become known as song form. Think of the popular songs you know; you may find that many of them are in ABA form!

Why is the structure on page 172, the Brandenburg Gate in Berlin, labeled ABA? Do you see that it has three sections? Do you see that the two end sections (the buildings) are alike and that the middle section (the columned gate) is different?

What is the form of "A Mighty Fortress Is Our God," on page 276? What is the form of "By the Waters of Babylon," on page 171? And how about "You're Never Fully Dressed Without a Smile" on page 109? Its form is . . . ?

Now listen to this well-known march. Can you figure out its form? Careful, it's complicated.

 Washington Post March . . . . Sousa

Can you identify the form of this song? The sections have been labeled to help you recognize them.

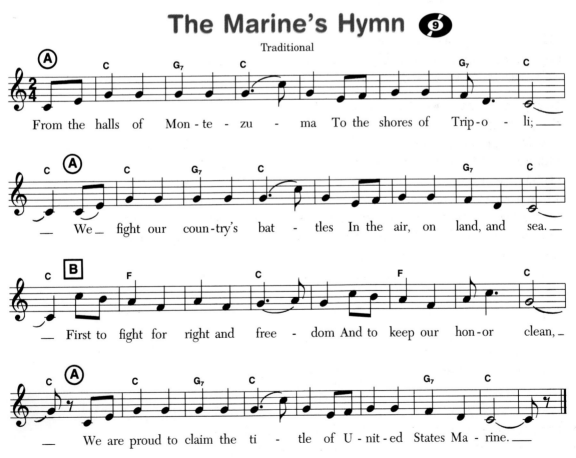

Courtesy of the United States Marine Corps

Rondo—Music's Bad Penny

"He's always turning up, just like a bad penny." You may have heard of people who would disappear for awhile but would eventually show up after a time. A *rondo* is like that. Do you hear anything recurring in this march?

 Colonel Bogey March . . . . Alford

After a short introduction you should have heard section A, section B, a return of A, then a totally *new* section, section C. Listen again and follow the chart to find out what happens next. (Of course, unlike the "bad penny," we greet each return of A with increasing delight.)

Introduction   **Interlude**

A Rondo by Beethoven

If you have studied piano for more than a few years, you may have played this well-known piano piece. As you listen to it, follow the Call Chart to hear the rondo form.

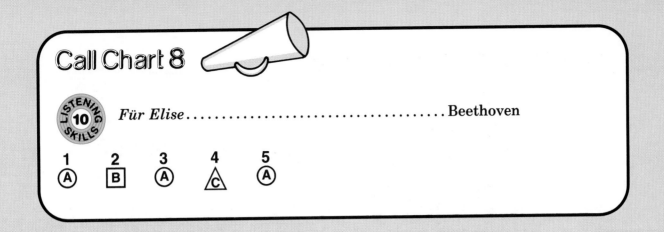

Call Chart 8

Für Elise . . . . Beethoven

1 (A) 2 [B] 3 (A) 4 △C 5 (A)

Now, here's a rondo to sing. Try "Dodi Li."

Dodi Li

Words Traditional   Music by Nira Chen   English Words by Dav ben Shmuel

A *Solo*

For — my — love   is   a   shep - herd — tend - ing — flocks
Do - di — li   va - 'a - ni — lo — ha - ro - e
doh - dee   lee   vah - ah - nee   loh   hah - roh - ay

B   *Chorus*

a - mong the fields.   Who is com - ing — from the wil - der - ness?
ba - sho - sha - nim.   All per - fumed — with — myrrh and frank - in - cense,
bah-shoh-shah-neem   Mi — zot   o - la — min — ha - mid - bar
                         mee   zoht   oh - lah   meen   hah-meed-bahr

A *Solo*

Who   is   fair   to — see?   For — my — love
She, my bride to — be.   Do - di — li
mi — zot   o - la.   doh - dee   lee
mee   zoht   oh - lah

is   a   shep - herd — tend - ing — flocks   a - mong the fields.
va - 'a - ni — lo — ha - ro - e   ba - sho - sha - nim.
vah - ah - nee   loh   hah - roh - ay   bah-shoh-shah-neem

Minuet .... Bach

Listen to this minuet and follow the music. You will see that there are boxes around some of the notes. By looking and listening you should be able to tell if the intervals are *steps, leaps,* or *repeats.* Write your answer in the box by putting S for step, L for Leap, and R for repeat.

Minuet

by J. S. Bach

Test 6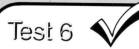

Write the letter of the correct answer in the blank.

1. Melodies move by _____ , _____ , and _____ .
   a. step
   b. reverse
   c. leap
   d. repeat

2. A major scale is a pattern of whole steps and _____ .
   a. half backs
   b. half beats
   c. whole notes
   d. half steps

3. A key signature shows what _____ are needed.
   a. sharps or naturals
   b. sharps or flats
   c. heels or flats
   d. flats or naturals

4. A minor scale sounds different from a major scale because it has a different _____ .
   a. step pattern
   b. melody
   c. key signature
   d. rhythm

5. A scale of only five notes, with a step-and-a-half between the third and fourth notes is called _____ .
   a. a pentatonic scale
   b. a twelve-tone scale
   c. a fish scale
   d. a chromatic scale

6. In a *sequence,* a melodic pattern is repeated _____ .
   a. at higher or lower levels
   b. once
   c. backwards
   d. with other instruments

7. In music, an interval is the span between two _____ .
   a. rests
   b. key signatures
   c. notes
   d. bar lines

8. "This Land Is Your Land" was written by _____ .
   a. Arlo Guthrie
   b. Tyrone Guthrie
   c. Woody Guthrie
   d. Frederick Guthrie

Test 7 ✔

Circle T if the statement is true; circle F if the statement is false.

1. When every other beat is accented, it is called meter in 3.

T   F

2. A meter signature shows how many notes are in each measure.

T   F

3. In a meter of 4, the accent falls on the first of every four beats.

T   F

4. When different meters follow each other in a beat, it is called *multimeter*.

T   F

5. In notation, the largest note unit is the sixteenth note.

T   F

Circle T if the statement is true; circle F if the statement is false.

1. When three notes are squeezed into the space of two, they are called trios.

T   F

2. A well-known American composer who wrote many rags at the beginning of the twentieth century was William Billings.

T   F

3. The word *accelerando* means "getting faster."

T   F

4. Harmony is the sounding of two or more tones together.

T   F

5. The way a voice or instrument sounds is called its *tone color*.

T   F

Test 9 ✓

Circle the correct answer.

1. A pattern that repeats over and over.

music   ostinato

2. In *In the Hall of the Mountain King,* Grieg repeats this over and over.

the melody   the orchestration

3. A Romantic-period style saw the use of it.

folk music   harpsichord music

4. Some metric patterns are in 5, 7, even 10! In your book, Sol Berkowitz wrote an arrangement of Stephen Foster's "Oh, Susanna." What meter was it in?

3   5   7   10

5. Some meters, like $\frac{6}{8}$ or $\frac{12}{8}$, are often thought of as being "inside" other meters. What are these meters called?

complex meters   simple meters   compound meters

6. Music is usually given shape by repetition and contrast of sections. This is called.

harmony   ostinato   riffs   form

7. An often-used form that is diagramed as ABACA has this name.

song form   rondo   sonata-allegro   ABA

PERFORMING MUSIC

The conductor enters to resounding applause. He may ask the orchestra to rise and share the accolade with him or her. The audience will not applaud again until after the piece is finished, not even after individual movements within the piece. The contrast between the silence during the performance and the clamor at the end is drama in itself.

Do you remember singing "Ode to Joy," on page 135? Try singing it again, and then listen to the way it is used in this selection, the finale to Beethoven's *Ninth Symphony.*

 Symphony No. 9 in D Minor, Movement 4 (excerpt)......
....Beethoven

That was quite a performance! In contrast, there is the soloist making music all alone. Listen to Jill Trinka, a teacher and folk singer, sing an old folk song, *Johnny Has Gone for a Soldier,* accompanying herself on the mountain dulcimer.

 Johnny Has Gone for a Soldier ..... American Folk Song

Building an Ensemble

Here is a line from a song that could be sung by a soloist.

Let's add another part. Of course, now it is no longer a solo, it's a *duet*.

Add another part and the song becomes a *trio*—an ensemble of three performers, like the song, "Laredo," on page 186.

Try singing "Laredo." Usually, when there are three parts, they are divided between two staffs to make them easier to read. In "Laredo," however, the three parts are all on one staff so you can best see their relationship. If the three parts are hard to sing together at first, work them out one at a time. You can build them up just the way a bricklayer lays bricks—one layer at a time.

Laredo

Mexican Folk Song   English Words by Margaret Marks

1. I'm off for La-re-do, fare-well my love, I'm sor-ry to cause you
2. I've brought you a hand-sewn sad-dle, my love, A blan-ket and bri-dle

pain; I prom-ise to send a let-ter, my love, To say when we'll meet a-
fine; So when you go past the bunk-house, my love, The cow-boys will know you're

gain. Don't fol-low a-cross the prai-rie, my love, Don't
mine. I've brought you a key of sil-ver, my love, At-

fol-low me where I go, But wait till I send a
tached to a gold-en chain, To lock up your heart for-

mes-sage, my love, Till then I will miss you so.
ev-er, my love, If nev-er we meet a-gain.

A Popular Trio

A few years ago there was a very popular singing trio called the
Andrews Sisters. They were very well known for their movie
appearances and for their tireless efforts to entertain military units
overseas during World War II. Listen to this selection by Laverne,
Maxene, and Patti Andrews. A big hit at one time, it still shows off
a special close-harmony sound like that of "Laredo."

 Boogie-Woogie Bugle Boy . . . . **Prince and Ray**

Close Up the Ranks, Men!

Men can sing in close harmony, too. (Close harmony, by the way, just means harmony in which the chord tones are close together, giving it a very rich, bright sound. It is this 🎵 instead of this 🎵 .)

During the 1950s and early 1960s, a male quartet called the Hi-Los sang, like the Andrews Sisters, in close harmony. Of course, since there were four of them, they could sing an extra note in each chord. And by this time, harmony was much thicker in texture and often included notes in the chords that were *dissonant,* not in harmony with the chord. Listen to this group sing a pop version of an old black spiritual.

Swing Low, Sweet Chariot . . . . Black Spiritual

Two Parts—Duet and Chorus

Do you remember what a song for two vocal parts is called? If you said *duet,* you're right. Step up and win the prize at Coney Island! What's the prize? A chance to sing this familiar song about New York's well-known amusement park. If you sing it as a group (half the class on Voice 1, the other half on Voice 2), you've formed a *chorus!*

Coney Island Baby

Words and Music by Les Applegate

Your version of "Coney Island Baby" is arranged in two parts. If two more parts could be added, the song would be a quartet. "Coney Island Baby" is a staple of the barbershop quartet repertoire. When men or women sing in barbershop style, the melody is in the second voice from the top. The voice above the melody, the specific kinds of chord progressions, as well as the close harmony, gives the barbershop quartet its special sound. Listen to this one.

Coney Island Baby . . . . **Applegate**

It's All in the Family

On page 140 you learned that instruments come in four basic families—woodwinds, brass, percussion, and strings. You can form your own percussion ensemble. The score below calls for two tuned percussion instruments (glockenspiel and resonator bells), and a line is provided for untuned instruments (finger cymbals, clave, tambourines). You can see that the player of the untuned percussion instruments must change instruments during the piece. You can add instruments as you like so that as many can play as possible.

Beating the Blahs

Mary E. Hoffman (Adapted)

The People's Choice

Music, music, music. There doesn't seem to be any group of people anywhere on earth that hasn't developed a rich musical life. Whether among the Inuit (IH noo iht) in their frozen homeland far above the Arctic Circle or among the Jívaro (HEE vah roh) Indians deep in the steaming jungles of Brazil's Mato Grosso, music can be found. The groups sing, and they make instruments by hand from whatever materials are available. Listen to the drumming of a short piece by the Yorubas, a group you discussed on page 12.

Yoruba Dance . . . . Traditional African

An Unusual Instrument

In the West Indies of the early twentieth century, ships delivered oil in large steel drums. The island residents found many uses for the empty drums, including one use that has come to symbolize the West Indies—as instruments for the steel drum band. People found that hitting the steel drums in different ways produced different pitches and that smaller drums had a higher sound than larger ones did. The residents found that by denting the tops of the drums, they could produce a scale. Finally they realized that cutting the drum in half increased its resonance. Listen to a steel drum band.

Steel Drum Band—"El Merecumbe"

Sin ellos no hay fiesta!

(Without Them There's No Party!)

In Mexico a very special kind of ensemble developed. The musicians are called *mariachis* (mah ree AH chees) and their ensemble is called a mariachi band. The music they make takes on a special sound quite unlike anything else you may have heard. The instrumentation usually consists of violins, guitars, and trumpets. And, of course, the mariachis sing as well! You can find these groups wherever there is a celebration—a *fiesta*—playing their infectious folk and popular melodies and rhythms. Listen to this mariachi band perform *Cielito lindo*.

 Cielito lindo . . . . Traditional Mexican

The Sound of the Highlands

Think of Scotland and what do you think of? Kilts? Heather? Haunted castles on the heath? You might think of these things, and then you might think of the bagpipe. Of course, many European countries have bagpipes—including Ireland, Spain, and Czechoslovakia—but somehow the Scottish folk seem to have made it most their own.

The bagpipe is an ancient folk instrument. Mention was even made of it in imperial Rome! Although the bagpipe looks complicated, it is really rather simple. The large bag is a bellows that blows air through the pipes. The player holds the bag under his or her arm and squeezes to get the air moving. The long pipe in the player's mouth is *not* what makes the sound. The player blows into the pipe to keep a steady supply of air in the bag. The sounding pipe is the small one fingered by the player. And the large pipes? You might think that they provide harmony, and they do, in a way. But they only play *one* pitch each—they are drones. It is this combination of drone and melody that gives the bagpipe that unique sound that many call "the sound of the highlands."

Listen to this bagpipe player.

Bagpipe Music—"Barren Rocks of Aden" and "Scotland, the Brave"..................................Traditional

And All That Jazz!

You have probably sung or heard this song before. Sing it now.

When the Saints Go Marching In

Black Spiritual

2. Oh, when the stars refuse to shine, . . .

3. Oh, when I hear that trumpet sound, . . .

The people of New Orleans developed a very special kind of ensemble—the Dixieland band. In Dixieland jazz, the melody is played by everyone, and then each player in turn improvises on the melody while all the others provide a little harmonic support. It is polite to applaud after each solo. Dixieland bands are not usually very large—five or six people at the most. Again, this style of ensemble playing has its own unique sound. Listen to what this group does with "When the Saints Go Marching In."

 When the Saints Go Marching In........Black Spiritual

The Dixieland band was one of the first jazz ensembles, and the jazz ensemble is still a very important part of the music scene. Listen to the Modern Jazz Quartet play a piece describing The Golden Striker, a figure on a clock tower in Venice. The instruments are piano, vibraphone, string bass, and percussion. Listen for the finger cymbals played at various times.

 The Golden Striker, "No Sun in Venice" ....Lewis

A Classic Jazz Ensemble

Among the jazz musicians of the last few years, a certain few names ring like no others—Charlie "Bird" Parker, Stan Kenton, Miles Davis, Pete Fountain, Al Hirt, Dave Brubeck, Chuck Mangione, Chick Corea. Dave Brubeck and his quartet were one of the most popular jazz ensembles for a long time. His experiments with rhythm and meter (Remember *Unsquare Dance* on page 157?) took him out of conventional jazz playing and made him one of the most influential jazz musicians.

Listen to the Dave Brubeck Quartet play *Camptown Races*. The instruments are piano, saxophone, bass, and percussion. You will hear that both the piano and the saxophone get a chance to improvise on the melody. Improvisation? You've heard that word before. That's what jazz is all about. You've heard it in each jazz piece you've listened to.

LISTENING SKILLS 11 *Camptown Races* . . . . Foster/Brubeck

The Vocal Backups

You've heard them. The singer appears live on a talk show or a recent rock video and sings his or her latest hit (or flop). Suddenly, from nowhere, you hear voices with the singer. Do they come from the beyond? More likely from the recording studio. These are backup singers. They are heard on the accompaniment tape (the "track" tape) that the singer uses when appearing on television. They're part of the arrangement. Sometimes they may sing words. At other times they may sing neutral syllables, such as *ah* or *oo*.

You can add vocal parts behind an existing composition. Listen to this piece by Philip Glass. You will notice that the music seems to change very little. Repetition is an important device for building a composition in this style, called *minimalism* (so called because the minimalist composer tries to create works using the minimal of materials). This music is a little like watching a lake in which the same small wave motions repeat over and over, changing only slightly. Listen to Glass' "A Gentleman's Honor" from his stage production *The Photographer*. There are only a few ideas repeated again and again.

 The Photographer, "A Gentleman's Honor"........Glass

You could probably hear slight variations as the piece went on. The one unchanging element was the eight-measure chord pattern:

A min. | A min. | F maj. | F maj. | G | G₇ | A min. | A min. |

You can do a vocal backup to the piece by singing the progression.

Of course you will need some words and rhythm to make it effective. Try

Or you might try

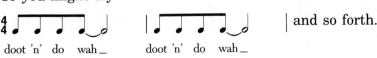 | and so forth.

Think up some rhythm patterns of your own. There are many that will fit.

"There are so many things going on! How can it all be kept together?"

Yes, for many it is mystifying how a composer deals with all those vocal and instrumental parts at all. But in music there are several ways to keep track of what's happening. Here's the melody of a song.

Young Person's Guide to the Orchestra — Benjamin Britten.
© Copyright 1946 by Hawkes and Son (London) Ltd.;
Renewed 1973. Reprinted by permission of Boosey & Hawkes, Inc.

Glee Reigns in Galilee
(Gilu Hagalilim)

Hebrew Folk Song   English Words by Dav ben Shmuel

Here's the same song with piano accompaniment. Remember the voice part is always on the top line, so it's easy to keep your place.

Be joy - ful,
Gi - lu   ha -
ghee - loo   hah -

Ga - li - le - ans,   raise   up   your   voic - es;   Be glad,   be   joy - ful____
ga - li - lim   gi - bo - rei   he - cha - yil;   Si - su   v' - sim - chu____
gah - lee - leem   ghee - boh - rai   heh - khah - yeel   see - soo   vuh - seem - khoo

morn - ing   and   eve - ning.   Be   joy - ful,   Ga - li - le - ans,   raise   up   your
yo - mam   va - la - yil.   Gi - lu   ha - ga - li - lim   gi - bo - rei   he -
yoh - mahm   vah - lah - yeel.   ghee - loo   hah - gah - lee - leem   ghee - boh - rai   heh -

voic - es;   Be glad,   be   joy - ful____   morn - ing   and   eve - ning.
cha - yil   Si - su   v' - sim - chu____   yo - mam   va - la - yil.
khah - yeel   See - soo   vuh - seem - khoo   yoh - mahm   vah - lah - yeel.

The Full Score

A full score can be of many sizes, from the smallest trio or quartet to the most instrument-packed of orchestral pieces. In a full score each instrument of the ensemble is shown on its own staff. If there are four instruments, there are four staffs. If there are ninety instruments, there are ninety staffs. Obviously, the last score is going to be of considerable size! The full score of an opera can weigh a great deal unless the type is reduced quite a bit!

Look at the full score for an instrumental ensemble. It consists of flute, trumpet, trombone, percussion, and bass. You can see that, as on previous pages, the melody is highlighted in yellow, even as it skips from instrument to instrument.

Glee Reigns in Galilee
(Gilu Hagalilim)
Hebrew Folk Song

Pass the Theme, Please!

Composers often like to pass a theme from one instrument or voice
to another. Being able to read a score is very important in helping
to keep track of these wandering themes. In this score the arrows
will help you keep track of where you are as the melody passes from
voice to voice. (Remember "Glee Reigns in Galilee" on page 202?)

Let It Snow

Words by Sammy Cahn   Music by Jule Styne   Arranged by Daniel Shigo

You Can't Tell the Players Without a Score

Look at the opening page of the full score for Benjamin Britten's *Young Person's Guide to the Orchestra.*

This is what the score looks like when it shows all the instruments. The woodwinds are at the top in green, the brass are next in red, then come the percussion instruments in yellow, and the strings are at the bottom in blue. Why, do you suppose, are the strings at the bottom in an orchestral score? Because when orchestras first began to organize, they were most commonly strings-only orchestras. As other instruments were added, they were placed on staffs above the strings.

Young Person's Guide to the Orchestra   BENJAMIN BRITTEN.

Young Person's Guide to the Orchestra — Benjamin Britten.
© Copyright 1946 by Hawkes and Son (London) Ltd;
Renewed 1973. Reprinted by permission of Boosey & Hawkes, Inc.

Call Chart 9

Listen to a Call Chart and find the appropriate instrument group in the score. Remember those colors. It will help you find them.

Young Person's Guide to the Orchestra,
"Introduction" ....Britten

1 Full orchestra

2 Woodwinds

3 Brass

4 Strings

5 Percussion

6 Full orchestra

Benjamin Britten
(1913–1976)

Benjamin Britten has been hailed by some as Great Britain's greatest composer since Henry Purcell, a Baroque-period composer. His many vocal and instrumental pieces have charmed the listening public since he first gained acclaim as a young prodigy. Perhaps his best known works are his operas, of which *Peter Grimes* is considered his masterpiece. Several other stage works, including *A Midsummer Night's Dream* and the spooky *The Turn of the Screw*, are widely performed.

Britten's output has also included a great deal of instrumental as well as non-operatic vocal music. His chamber music works with voice, such as *Serenade for Tenor, Horn, and Strings*, are considered by many to be among the finest small ensemble writing in the twentieth century. And his large choral pieces, such as *A Ceremony of Carols* and *War Requiem*, have been hailed by critics as contemporary masterpieces.

Careers in Music—Conducting

A conductor must be on the ball to keep track of all those instruments. Listen to what one prominent conductor, Eve Queler, has to say about conducting.

 11 *Careers in Music—Eve Queler*

 11 *Le Cid,* "Aragonaise" .... Massenet

A Theme Musical by Carmino Ravosa

Want to put on a show? You can, you know. You'll find all the makings of a show right here on the next few pages. The script will give you a beginning, an end, and a hook (a unifying idea that catches an audience's attention). Your show can be big or small. You can follow the script, using the songs suggested, or you can use other songs from elsewhere in the book or even from outside the book.

For staging you can use a few multilevel boxes, perhaps painted in vivid colors. Use your imagination. Just remember, you and the songs are the most important parts of the show!

(Stage is empty . . . lush instrumental music is heard playing "Don't Go Anywhere Without a Song" as a student makes his or her way on stage.)

STUDENT: Our show is all about songs. There's no scenery, and no costumes . . . just songs with a few words in between to tie them together.

There's magic in songs. Whether you're sad, happy, bored, down, blue, whether you feel like quitting or you're on top of the world, there's a song that's just right to express your feeling. So—don't go anywhere without a song!

(As the song is sung, performers appear from all over the auditorium and take their places on stage.)

Don't Go Anywhere Without a Song ⑪

Words and Music by Carmino Ravosa

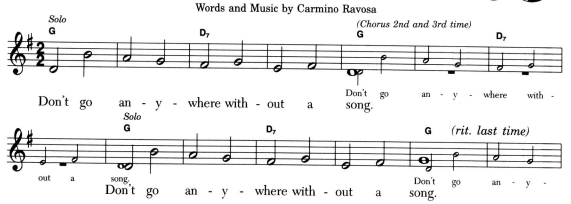

where with - out a song.

Don't get caught with - out _____ one.
If you're caught in traf - fic

Who knows what life will bring? Wher - ev - er you may
or if you're feel - ing ill. A song is sure to

be. _____ Have a song to sing.
help. _____ If there's an - y thing that will. song.

Now go into any songs you'd like. Just write your own lead-in. For
example: "Sometimes you get caught up in school, rushing around,
working, trying to save time. Here's how one songwriter felt about
time."

Song: "Time in a Bottle," page 300

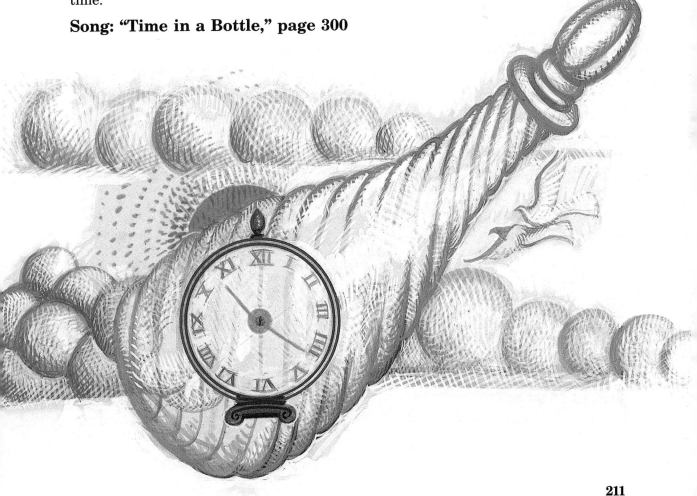

STUDENT: When people get up in the morning, they put on their slacks or skirts, or perhaps their jeans, a shirt, socks, shoes—and now they're ready for the day, right?

Wrong! You're not fully dressed yet. Go back to the mirror.

Song: "You're Never Fully Dressed Without a Smile," page 109

STUDENT: Got a good friend? When's the last time you told him (her) how important he (she) was?

Song: "I'd Do Anything," page 230

STUDENT: Before you can like others or just one special person, you've got to like yourself first. And, you know, I've got some philosophy on that.

I Like Me

Words and Music by Carmino Ravosa

Solo 1st time, chorus 2nd time

If I can smile ___ and do some-thing worth-while, ___ I like me.

If I can give ___ ev-'ry day that I live, ___ I like me.

If I can boast ___ that I've giv-en my most, ___ I like me. If

each day I plan ___ to give some-one a hand, ___ I like me. If I can

look at my-self ___ in the mir-ror each night ___ and I learn the dif-

- f'rence be-tween wrong and right, ___ Then I can say ___ at the

end of each day ___ I like me. me.

STUDENT: And when friendship really clicks, it's wonderful. There's nothing quite like a really good friend. When a friend is around, you can bet everything's coming up roses.

Everything's Coming Up Roses

Words by Stephen Sondheim   Music by Jule Styne

Things look swell,   Things look great,   Gon - na
Clear the decks,   Clear the tracks,   We got

have the whole world___ on a plate.   Start - ing
noth - ing to do___ but re - lax,   Blow a

here,___ Start - ing now,___ hon - ey,
kiss,___ Take a bow,___ hon - ey,

Ev - 'ry - thing's com - ing___ up ros - es!
Ev - 'ry - thing's com - ing___ up ros - es!

Now's our___ in - ning.___ Stand the world on its ear!_

Set it___ spin - ning___ That -'ll be just the be -

gin - ning!___ Cur - tain up! Light the lights!

We got noth - ing to hit___ but the heights!

We'll be swell,___ We'll be great! ___ I can tell,___

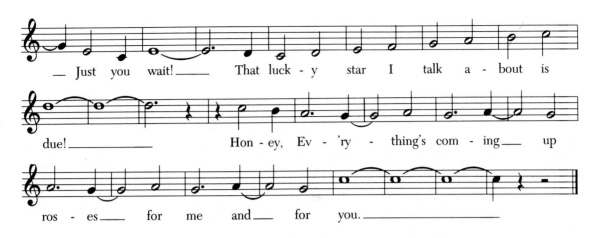

— Just you wait! _____ That luck-y star I talk a-bout is

due! _____ Hon-ey, Ev-'ry-thing's com-ing _____ up

ros-es _____ for me and _____ for you. _____

STUDENT: Sometimes it feels as if you have no friends at all. When you feel like quitting something . . . I guess we all face that sometimes . . . there must be a song for that kind of feeling.

Never Say Never 🎵⑪

Words and Music by Carmino Ravosa

Nev-er _ say nev-er, _ Nev-er _ say die. Yes, you _ can do it, _ that's if _ you try.

Don't be _ a quit-ter _ and some day _ you'll win; Don't you _ give up and _ don't you _ give

in. Nev-er _ say nev-er, _ Nev-er _ say no, There is _ no doubt you _ can

do it, _ I know. _____ Nev-er _ say nev - er. _

CHAPTER 9—OLIVER!

When *Oliver!* premiered in London in the early 1960s, and later on Broadway, it was an instant success. Many critics had felt that the stories of Charles Dickens were too highbrow for the popular theater. *Oliver!* proved them wrong. The score by Lionel Bart was attractive and inventive to many, and the show paved the way for other Dickens-inspired musicals on Broadway, in the movies, and on television. *Oliver!* proved that there is no subject that cannot be discussed on the Broadway stage.

Here is a kind of concert version of *Oliver!* that you and your classmates can perform. All you need is a narrator (if you use several, it is more interesting), a record player, and your own voice.

It will be effective to have some students mime the action. That is, act it out without words.

The Story of Oliver Twist

NARRATOR: In England the Poor Law of 1834 said that all able-bodied paupers must live in a workhouse. Families were separated. Hunger and abuse were common. In Britain during the early nineteenth century, poverty was considered a crime!

11 *Overture*

ACT I, SCENE 1
SETTING: A workhouse for paupers and orphans.
(As music begins, children enter the room single file, moving toward assigned table locations. With all in place at tables, song begins.)

Food, Glorious Food ⑪

Words and Music by Lionel Bart

Slowly

All:

Food,   glo - ri - ous food!   Hot   sau - sage and mus - tard;

While   we're in   the mood,   Cold   jel - ly and cus - tard!

All

Pease   pud - ding and sa - ve - loys,   "What   next?" is the ques - tion.

All

Rich   gen - tle - men have   it,   boys: In - dye - ges - tion!

Food,   glo - ri - ous food!   We're   an - xious to   try   it;

Three   ban - quets a   day,   our   fa - vor - ite   di - et.

Just   pic - ture a great   big   steak,   fried,   roast - ed   or stewed!   Oh,

1st Boy · *All* · *2nd Boy* · *All* · *rall.*

Food,   won - der - ful food,   mar - ve - lous   food,   glo - ri - ous

Faster

food! ____

1. Food,   glo - ri - ous   food, ____
2. Food,   glo - ri - ous   food, ____

What is ____ there more hand-some? ____ Gulped, swal - lowed, or chewed, ____
Don't care ___ what it looks like! ____ Burned, un - der-done, crude, ____

Still worth ____ a king's ran - som! ____ What is ____ it we
Don't care ____ what it cooks like! ____ Just think - ing of

dream a - bout, ____ what brings ____ on a sigh? _____ Piled peach -
grow - ing fat, ____ our sens - es go reel - ing ____ One mo -

1st Boy

All

- es and cream, a - bout six feet high! _____ Food, glo -
- ment of know - ing that full - up feel - ing! ____ Food, glo -

- ri - ous food, ____ eat right ____ through the men - u.
- ri - ous food, ____ what would - n't we give for ____

Just loos - en your belt ____ Two inch - es and then you ____
that ex - tra bit more? ____ That's all ____ that we live for. ____

Work up ____ a new ap - pe - tite ____ in this ___ in - ter -
Why should ____ we be fat - ed to ____ do no - thing but

2nd Boy   *All*   *3rd Boy*

lude, then, food, once ____ a - gain, food, fa - bu - lous
brood on food, no - thing but food, ma - gi - cal

food, glo - ri - ous food! _____

food, beau - ti - ful food, glo - ri - ous food! _____

(At the close of the song, Mr. Bumble walks onto the upper level; children turn their heads in his direction.)

NARRATOR 2: Mr. Bumble, the parish beadle, strides onto the upper level of the workhouse, accompanied by Widow Corney, the matron of the workhouse. He holds his mace in a taunting manner as all eyes turn toward him in fear. When the mace strikes the floor, the children file slowly to the vats of gruel, receive one ladle-ful, and return to their seats. Once seated, they remain motionless, awaiting the signal to begin eating. Bumble deliberately waits to strike the mace upon the floor, knowing that they are almost starved, and enjoying his position of authority.

NARRATOR 1: The meager rations are quickly devoured. All eyes now turn toward one of the children—Oliver—who slowly picks up his bowl, rises, and hesitantly approaches Mr. Bumble. (It seems that Oliver has been selected as a representative of the children to request more food!) Everyone waits and watches in silence as Oliver asks for *more to eat*! Mr. Bumble goes into a furious rage and calls for his helpers to seize Oliver and lock him up!

• F O R   S T U D Y •

Can you provide background music or appropriate sounds during or following the preceding narration? Remember that your music must enhance or add to the drama, the expressiveness, and the excitement. Weave your music between the narration; do not overpower or drown out the speaker.

NARRATOR 2: Before the second scene, Mr. Bumble and Widow Corney have decided that Oliver is a troublemaker and plan to get rid of him. With his belongings wrapped in a small bundle, Oliver is led onto the streets by Mr. Bumble, who hawks him for sale to the highest bidder.

Boy for Sale (Mr. Bumble)

SCENE 2

SETTING: *The upper level has a door with a sign reading Sowerberry Funeral Home. The lower level is a funeral workroom with coffins, bucket, mop, scrub brush, and a dog's bowl.*

• FOR STUDY •

Can you prepare music for this scene, to be included before the song "Where Is Love"? How will you express musically Oliver's feelings in this situation? Which instruments will best provide the mood? In which direction should the melodic line move? Consider the tempo, dynamic levels, and rhythmic patterns of your composition.

NARRATOR 1: Eventually Mr. Sowerberry, an undertaker, who is in need of an assistant, decides to take Oliver on a trial basis. He is assured by Mr. Bumble that Oliver will require very little food and will work hard for his keep. Sowerberry immediately puts Oliver to work, gives him the remains of food in the dog's bowl as his meal, and sends him to the downstairs room where coffins are stored. Oliver's song, "Where is Love?", on page 222, is the theme and essence of the Dickens novel. Oliver reflects on his search for love.

Where Is Love?

Words and Music by Lionel Bart

Where _____ is love? Does it fall from skies a-
bove? Is it un-der-neath the wil-low tree _____ that
I've been dream-ing of? Where _____ is she
Who I close my eyes to see? Will I ev-er know that
sweet "hel-lo" _____ that's meant for on-ly me?
Who can say where she may hide? Must I tra-vel far and wide,
Till I am be-side the some-one who I can mean
some-thing to? Where, _____ where _____ is
love? Who can say where she may hide?

Must I tra-vel far and wide, Till I am be-side the some-one who I can mean some-thing to? Where, _____ where _____ is love? _____

rit.

NARRATOR 2: Noah Claypole, a bully, who also works for Mr. Sowerberry, provokes Oliver into a fight by taunting him about his mother. To subdue him, Mrs. Sowerberry and her daughter, Charlotte, throw Oliver into a coffin. This upsets Mrs. Sowerberry and causes her to faint. As the others rush to Mrs. Sowerberry's aid, Oliver manages to escape from the undertaking establishment and moves toward another episode in his life.

SCENE 3

SETTING: *Fagin's den on one side, a road to London on other side of stage.*

NARRATOR 1: Alone, hungry, and friendless, Oliver has spent several days and nights on the roads leading to London. As he pauses on his journey to rest and finish the remains of a crust of bread, he is closely observed by an outlandishly dressed young man named Jack Dawkins, better known as the Artful Dodger. Dodger approaches Oliver, offers him an apple and an introduction to his boss, Fagin, who (he promises) will give Oliver food, a job, and a place to sleep.

Oliver finds it hard to believe that he has found a friend as Dodger assures him that he will be welcomed as one of the family. Perhaps Oliver is finally about to experience a turn for the better. Come with him now to discover if the change is for the better . . . or for the worse.

Consider Yourself

Words and Music by Lionel Bart

lar - der days,   why   grouse?   Al - ways a   chance we'll meet

some - bo - dy   to   foot   the   bill,   Then   the   drinks   are   on   the

house! ____   Con - si - der your-self   our   mate.   We

don't want to   have   no   fuss,   For   af - ter some con -

si - der - a - tion we   can   state: Con - si - der your-self   one   of

Oliver   *Dodger*

us!   Con - si - der your-self   At   home ____   Con -

Oliver   *Dodger*

si - der   your - self   One   of   the   fa - mi - ly.   We've

Oliver   *Dodger*   *Both*

ta - ken   to   you   So   strong   It's   clear   we're

Dodger   *Oliver*

go - ing   to   get   a - long.   Con - si - der your-self   Well

(All move to Fagin's den at close of song.)

• FOR STUDY •

Can you compose an appropriate theme or motive to be played
whenever Fagin appears or is referred to in the narration?
Remember, there is a tinge of humor and a theatrical flair in this
devious criminal!

NARRATOR 2: Once inside Fagin's den, as his abode is so aptly
named, Oliver is introduced to Fagin, the sly and crafty older
gentleman who runs a school for pickpockets and thieves. Oliver's
interest in Fagin's "business" (which to this point has not been
explained to Oliver) prompts Fagin and his students to describe
their work through song and pantomime. Oliver is even given a
chance to "try his hand" at their profession during this musical
number.

  You've Got to Pick a Pocket or Two

NARRATOR 1: When everyone has been fed and bedded down for the night, Fagin brings from a secret hiding place a chest filled with expensive jewels that he has managed to keep aside for himself. He delights in holding each piece and admiring its beauty. He revels in the fortune he has amassed for himself, and he feels the jewels may be his insurance for his later years or against unforeseen problems.

· FOR STUDY ·

You may want to consider snatches (or all) of "Fagin's Theme" interspersed throughout the above narration as an underscore.

NARRATOR 2: The next morning, everyone is aroused when Nancy and Bet arrive. Both are involved in Fagin's business. In addition, Nancy works as a waitress and is the girlfriend of Bill Sikes, who is feared and hated by all. Nancy is introduced to the new boy, Oliver, and immediately senses that his manners mark him as different from the rest. Here is a young gentleman!

NARRATOR 1: Nancy and Dodger—both of whom love to be on stage and have a definite flair for drama—decide they will show the group how proper ladies and gentlemen should act as they put on their airs of upper-crust society for all. *(Nancy and Dodger sing "I'd Do Anything," on page 230.)*

I'd Do Anything

Words and Music by Lionel Bart

NARRATOR 2: Within a few days, Oliver is sent off into the streets with Dodger to observe how successful pickpocketing is accomplished.

Outside a bookstore, Dodger skillfully removes a wallet from a wealthy gentleman's pocket.

Almost instantly the man realizes that his wallet is missing as he reaches to pay for a purchase.

Dodger makes a quick exit from the scene and the gentleman turns to see Oliver, looking both innocent and guilty at once.

Oliver hesitates, gathers his wits, and runs. He is thought to be the thief and is captured as Act One concludes.

ACT II, SCENE 1

LISTENING SKILLS 12 *Oom Pah Pah*

NARRATOR 1: As Act Two begins, Nancy is entertaining her customers with a rousing song, "Oom Pah Pah!". All join her as they beat time, move to the music, sing heartily, and applaud loudly.

NARRATOR 2: Suddenly the jovial atmosphere is hushed as everyone cowers and tries to hide in the shadows. Bill Sikes has entered the room! He brags of his brute strength and evil ways. He dares anyone to move or speak as he saunters about the room!

NARRATOR 1: The spell is broken as a breathless Dodger rushes in to inform Fagin, Sikes, and Nancy of Oliver's capture. He also relates that during the court trial, the bookseller who observed the crime absolved Oliver of any wrongdoing.

NARRATOR 2: And the wealthy gentleman, Mr. Brownlow, victim of the crime, has taken Oliver with him to his home!

NARRATOR 1: Both Sikes and Fagin realize that Oliver may talk and expose their operation to the law. They determine that Oliver must be taken from his benefactor. As their thoughts turn to who might best accomplish this deed, Sikes decides that Nancy could pull it off because Oliver trusts her friendship.

NARRATOR 2: When Nancy refuses and pleads that Oliver deserves this chance for a better life, Sikes strikes her and threatens to kill her.

NARRATOR 1: Left alone, Nancy sings a soliloquy that reveals her innermost feelings for Sikes and her need to love and be loved in return.

· FOR STUDY ·

Although the above narration is fast-moving, exciting, and loaded with conflicting emotions, it is lengthy. Here is an opportunity to incorporate music, sounds, or themes you have already composed or to add new music. Your music may occur within a narrator's segment or between narrations.

As Long as He Needs Me

Words and Music by Lionel Bart

SCENE 2

SETTING: *The lower level represents a street. The upper level shows the doorway entrance to Mr. Brownlow's house.*

(Vendors appear on the street with baskets of flowers, fruits, vegetables, pails of milk, and so on. Mr. Brownlow and Oliver stand at the doorway, observing.)

NARRATOR 2: At the Brownlow residence, Oliver is under excellent care, is in good health, is receiving an education, has fine clothing, and—finally—is loved.

NARRATOR 1: (A most interesting point to note at this time: Mr. Brownlow cannot remove from his mind the striking resemblance between Oliver and his own daughter, Agnes, who vanished approximately ten years ago).

NARRATOR 2: One beautiful day, Mr. Brownlow decides to send Oliver to the library to return some books. Everyone is caught up in the joy of this song as Oliver unknowingly walks into the trap Nancy has set for him.

Who Will Buy?

Words and Music by Lionel Bart

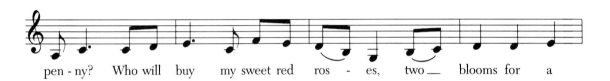

Rose Seller

Who will buy my sweet red ros - es, two __ blooms for a

pen - ny? Who will buy my sweet red ros - es, two __ blooms for a

pen - ny?

Milkmaid

Will you buy an - y milk to - day,

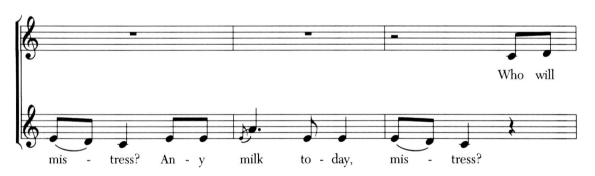

Who will

mis - tress? An - y milk to - day, mis - tress?

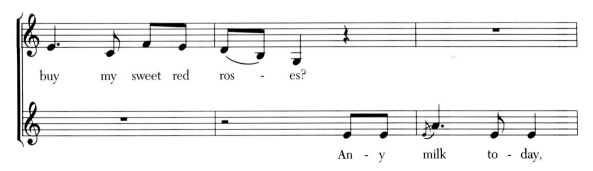

buy my sweet red ros - es?

An - y milk to - day,

sky you ne-ver did see!___ Who will tie it up with a rib-

All

-bon, and put it in a box for me? There'll nev-er

be a day so sun-ny,___ It could not hap-pen twice.

Where is the man with all the mon-ey?___ It's cheap at

half the price!___ Who will buy this won-der-ful morn - ing?

I'm so high, I swear I could fly.___ Me, oh my! I

Oliver Moderately

don't want to lose___ it! So what am I to do, to

a tempo

keep the sky so blue? There must be some-one who will buy!

Rose Seller

Who will buy my sweet red ros - es, two___ blooms for a pen-ny?

(At the end of the song, when the rose seller sings, Oliver begins to walk down the street. Nancy and Bet appear as Oliver innocently greets them.)

238

NARRATOR 1: Nancy pretends that Oliver is her lost brother, who ran away from home and broke his mother's heart. Her acting is so convincing that the crowd turns against Oliver and ignores his pleas that the whole scene is a sham.

NARRATOR 2: Sikes appears and he and Nancy hustle Oliver away to Fagin's hideout. Kidnapped! Once again, Oliver's life has taken a drastic turn!

SCENE 3:

SETTING: *Fagin's den. Nancy, Sikes, Oliver, Dodger, Fagin. Nancy standing apart from others, Sikes roughly holding Oliver, Dodger alongside Fagin. When narration concludes, Nancy angrily moves off, followed by Sikes pushing Oliver. Finally, Dodger walks off in same direction, leaving Fagin alone on stage.)*

NARRATOR 1: Nancy is upset over her role in the kidnapping of Oliver and is concerned with Sikes's rough treatment of the boy. She informs Fagin and Sikes that she will tell all she knows of their operation if they are not careful. Once Nancy parts from their company, Fagin warns Sikes to watch her closely.

NARRATOR 2: When Sikes is out of earshot, Fagin orders Dodger to follow him. (Fagin has never trusted Sikes. Even though they work together, they are mortal enemies.)

NARRATOR 1: Now alone, Fagin brings out his chest of jewels and contemplates this latest turn of events. In his song, he ponders what he now must consider for his own way of life . . . even a change to going honest!

When Fagin sends Dodger off to follow Sikes and stands alone with his chest of jewels, try using Fagin's theme as an underscore.

Reviewing the Situation 🔟

Words and Music by Lionel Bart

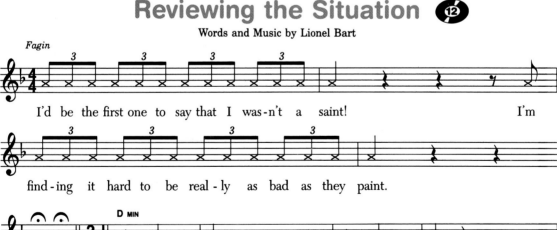

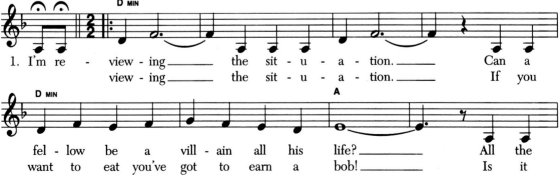

tri - als _____ and tri - bu - la - tion, _____ Bet - ter
such a _____ hu - mil - i - a - tion _____ for a

set - tle down and get my - self a wife. _____ And a
rob - ber to per - form an hon - est job? _____ So a

accel. poco a poco -

wife would cook and sew for me, and come for me and
job I'm get - ting poss - i - bly, I won - der who the

go for me (And go for me), and nag at me, The
boss - 'll be? Won - der if he'll take to me? What

fin - gers she will wag at me, The mon - ey she will
bon - us - es he'll make to me? I'll start at eight and

take from me, A mis - er - y she'll make from me. I
fin - ish late, At nor - mal rate, and all, but wait! I

1.
Tempo I

think I'd bet - ter think it out a - gain. _____ 2. I'm re -

Final verse

think I'll have to think it out a - gain. Hey!

241

NARRATOR 2: Meanwhile, back to the subplot in this adventure story. An old woman, Sally, who was present in the workhouse when a child was born to an inmate, has decided to unfold her long-kept secret to Mr. Bumble and Widow Corney before her death. (By the way, Mrs. Corney is now *Mrs. Bumble*!) Sally shows the locket she robbed from the child's dead mother and says that the dying woman's last words told of an inheritance for her child whose name was . . . *Oliver*!

NARRATOR 1: Mr. and Mrs. Bumble, in their greed, scheme to reclaim Oliver and thereby inherit his fortune for themselves. But Mr. Brownlow foils their plot when he becomes incensed over their treatment and sale of Oliver and threatens to have both of them fired from their positions. Upon opening the locket, Mr. Brownlow discovers that it contains a picture of his daughter Agnes. *He is Oliver's grandfather!*

NARRATOR 2: As the plot moves to a close, Nancy appears at Mr. Brownlow's residence and promises to bring Oliver to him at midnight on London Bridge.

(A bell strikes twelve times.)

NARRATOR 1: That night, as Nancy hurries Oliver to the appointed meeting, Bill Sikes stealthily follows and kills her. Mr. Brownlow appears just in time to see Sikes disappear with Oliver.

NARRATOR 2: As an angry crowd searches for Sikes, it batters in the door of Fagin's den, where Sikes has taken Oliver. Sikes pulls his hostage onto the roof in a desperate attempt to escape. He is discovered by the crowd, is shot, and falls to his death.

NARRATOR 1: In the meantime, Fagin and his pickpockets have been alerted and have managed to run to safety. The crowd emerges from Fagin's den, excitedly showing off his chest of precious jewels that it has uncovered. Oliver's grandfather, Mr. Brownlow, rescues Oliver and takes him home.

NARRATOR 2: Slowly, cautiously, from beneath the bridge where he has been hiding, Fagin emerges. Alone and contemplating his future once again, Fagin walks off as he sings: "Can somebody change? S'possible. Maybe it's strange—s'possible. All my dearest companions and treasures, I've left 'em behind. I'll turn a leaf over, and, who can tell what I may find?" Just before he exits, he turns toward us with a sly wink, a wry smile . . . and then disappears.

Finale—entire cast.

· F O R S T U D Y ·

A reprise of "Consider Yourself" and "I'd Do Anything" is suggested as the finale. You may prefer to arrange your own finale, coordinating music with the entrance of characters as they take curtain calls.

Audiences have fun in the theater. They laugh uproariously at the jokes and listen attentively to the songs, often applauding a song just as in an opera. If the dialogue is especially witty, they may even applaud that, as well.

What Do You Hear 3

 Young Person's Guide to the Orchestra, "Introduction" ... Britten

As you listen to the introduction to *Young Person's Guide to the Orchestra,* you will hear numbers called. At each number, look at the choice of answers. Circle the answer you think is correct.

1. Full orchestra   Clarinet and flute duet

2. Brass   Woodwinds

3. Organ   Brass

4. Strings   Drum

5. Percussion   Strings

6. Solo flute   Full orchestra

Test 10 ✓

Write the letter of the correct answer in the blank.

1. When you listened to "Johnny Has Gone for a Soldier" you heard a folk singer accompanying herself on the mountain _____.

   a. flute
       b. oboe
   c. dulcimer
    d. recorder

2. A group of people performing together is called _____.

   a. an ensemble
    b. a folk group
   c. a rock band
    d. a music club

3. A song for two vocal parts is called _____.

   a. a trio
      b. a symphony
   c. a choir
     d. a duet

4. A song for three vocal parts is called _____.

   a. a trio
      b. a symphony
   c. a choir
     d. a duet

5. The Hi-Los, a men's vocal group, use a kind of harmony called _____.

   a. right harmony
    b. close harmony
   c. real harmony
    d. instrumental harmony

6. A large group of voices is called _____.

   a. a solo
      b. a chorus
   c. an orchestra
    d. a flutist

Test 11 ✓

Write the letter of the correct answer in the blank.

1. You learned that instruments are grouped in families. The violin
   is a part of the _____ family.

   a. woodwind   b. string
   c. brass   d. percussion

2. The flute is a member of the _____ family.

   a. woodwind   b. string
   c. brass   d. percussion

3. The bass drum is a member of the _____ family.

   a. woodwind   b. string
   c. brass   d. percussion

4. The trumpet is a member of the _____ family.

   a. woodwind   b. string
   c. brass   d. percussion

5. The clarinet is a member of the _____ family.

   a. woodwind   b. string
   c. brass   d. percussion

6. The cymbals are a member of the _____ family.

   a. woodwind   b. string
   c. brass   d. percussion

7. The trombone is a member of the _____ family.

   a. woodwind   b. string
   c. brass   d. percussion

8. The cello is a member of the _____ family.

   a. woodwind   b. string
   c. brass   d. percussion

Test 12 ✔

Write the letter of the correct answer in the blank.

1. Many groups of people have special instruments. The Yoruba, of Africa, play a great deal on _____ .

   a. bagpipes
   c. guitars
   b. percussion instruments
   d. flutes

2. Steel drums are associated with the people of _____ .

   a. New England
   c. the West Indies
   b. Japan
   d. New York City

3. An ensemble of musicians in Mexico that includes guitars, trumpets, and violins is called _____ .

   a. a mariachi band
   c. the Latin American Ensemble
   b. the Mexico City Philharmonic
   d. the Mexico Group

4. The instrument most closely associated with Scotland is _____ .

   a. the bagpipe
   c. the guitar
   b. the snare drum
   d. the flute

5. In New Orleans a style of jazz was developed called _____ .

   a. hot
   c. Dixieland
   b. New York-style
   d. St. Louis

Test 13 ✔

Write the letter of the correct answer in the blank.

1. A modern style that reduces harmony and melody to simple repetition is called _____ .

   a. neo-Baroque
   c. minimalism
   b. expressionism
   d. impressionism

2. The music that shows all the instruments or voices of a composition is called a _____ .

   a. line
   c. staff
   b. page
   d. score

3. Orchestra scores can be very complicated looking on the page. Often each instrument will have its own staff. If there are 18 different instruments, there will be _____ .

   a. an intermission
   c. 18 staffs
   b. two conductors
   d. three flutists

4. Because other instruments were added to the Baroque string orchestra, their parts are always notated _____ the strings.

   a. above
   b. below

5. In her interview, conductor Eve Queler places a great deal of importance to a conductor on _____ .

   a. reading books
   c. training
   b. traveling
   d. singers

Test 14 ✓

Circle T if the statement is true; circle F if the statement is false.

1. *Oliver* is based on the story of Oliver Twist, by William Shakespeare.

    T   F

2. In Act I, the orphans are living in a palatial estate.

    T   F

3. The first song they sing is "Food, Glorious Food."

    T   F

4. Mr. Bumble sells Oliver to Mr. Sowerberry, an undertaker.

    T   F

5. Oliver escapes from Mr. Sowerberry and meets a boy called the Artful Codger.

    T   F

6. After being taken into Fagin's "business" Oliver is befriended by a young woman named Nancy, who is Fagin's girlfriend.

    T   F

7. Oliver is taken in by a wealthy gentleman, but is kidnapped by Bill Sikes.

    T   F

8. After Oliver's capture, Bill Sikes is chased onto a roof with Oliver and is allowed to go free.

    T   F

SING AND CELEBRATE

All for the Best

from *Godspell*

Words and Music by Stephen Schwartz

America

Words by Samuel Francis Smith Music by Henry Carey

1. My coun - try! 'tis of thee, Sweet land of
2. My na - tive coun - try, thee, Land of the
3. Let mu - sic swell the breeze, And ring from
4. Our fa - ther's God, to thee, Au - thor of

lib - er - ty, Of thee I sing; Land where my
no - ble free, Thy name I love; I love thy
all the trees, Sweet free - dom's song; Let mor - tal
lib - er - ty, To thee we sing; Long may our

fa - thers died, Land of the Pil - grims' pride,
rocks and rills, Thy woods and tem - pled hills,
tongues a - wake, Let all that breathe par - take,
Land be bright, with free - dom's ho - ly light,

From ev - 'ry__ moun - tain - side, Let__ free - dom ring!
My heart_ with_ rap - ture thrills Like__ that a - bove.
Let rocks_ their_ si - lence break, The__ sound pro - long.
Pro - tect_ us_ by thy might, Great_ God, our King!

Dona nobis pacem

Words Traditional Music by Allen Brings

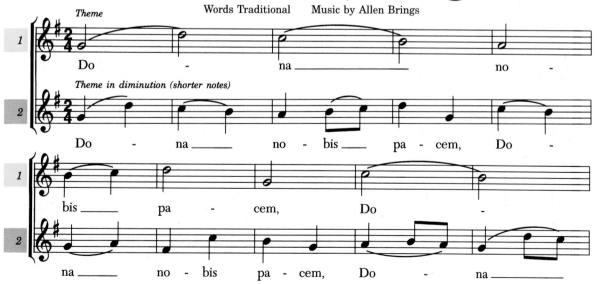

Theme

1 Do - na__ no -

Theme in diminution (shorter notes)

2 Do - na__ no - bis_ pa - cem, Do -

1 bis__ pa - cem, Do -

2 na__ no - bis pa - cem, Do - na__

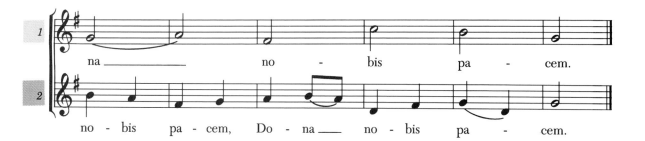

na _____ no - bis pa - cem.

no - bis pa - cem, Do - na ___ no - bis pa - cem.

Erie Canal

American Folk Song

1. I got a ___ mule, her name is ___ Sal,
2. Git up there, Sal, we passed that ___ lock,

Fif - teen ___ miles on the

E - rie Ca - nal! ___ She's a good old ___ work - er and a good old ___ pal,
And ___ we'll make Rome ___ 'fore ___ six o' - clock,

Fif - teen ___ miles on the E - rie Ca - nal! ___ We've hauled some barg - es
Just one more trip and

in our ___ day, Filled with lum - ber, coal, and ___ hay, And
back we'll ___ go Through the rain and sleet and ___ snow, 'Cause

we know ev - 'ry inch of the way From Al - ba - ny ___ to ___ Buf - fa - lo. ___
we know ev - 'ry inch of the way

REFRAIN
Chorus

Low bridge, ev - 'ry - bod - y down, Low bridge, 'cause we're com - ing to a town; And you'll

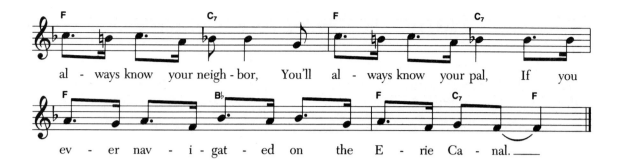

al - ways know your neigh - bor, You'll al - ways know your pal, If you

ev - er nav - i - gat - ed on the E - rie Ca - nal. _____

Gaudeamus omnes in Domino 🔘12

Plainsong

Gau - de - a - mus om - nes _ in _ Do - mi - no, _
gow - day - ah - moos ohm - nehs een doh - mee - noh

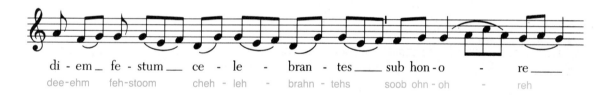

di - em _ fe - stum _ ce - le - bran - tes _____ sub hon - o - re _____
dee - ehm feh - stoom cheh - leh - brahn - tehs soob ohn - oh - reh

sanc - to - rum _____ om - ni - um: de _ quo - rum sol - em - ni - ta -
sahnk - toh - room ohm - nee - oom day qwoh - room sohl - ehm - nee - tah -

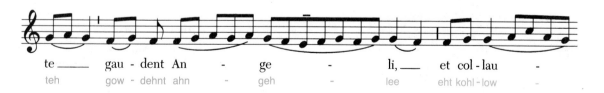

te _____ gau - dent An - ge - li, _____ et col - lau -
teh gow - dehnt ahn - geh - lee eht kohl - low -

dant _ Fi - li - um _____ De - i. _____
dahnt fee - lee - oom day - ee

Here We Come A-Singing

Words and Music by David Eddleman

Cel - e-brate the sto-ry they told _ of the eight-day mir-a-cle of old. _____

Cel - e-brate the sto-ry they told _ of the eight-day mir-a-cle of old. _____

Fes-ti - val of sing - ing and fes-ti - val of joy, cheer-ing ev'-ry hap - py

Sing the fes - ti - val of joy, cheer - ing ev'- ry

girl and boy; Spin the drey - dl, light the me-nor - ah, time that we all en -

girl and boy; Spin the drey - dl, light the me-nor - ah, time that we all en -

cresc. *(opt. div.)*

joy. Spin the drey - dl, light the me-nor - ah, cel - e-brate this Ha - nuk-kah

cresc. *(div.)*

joy. Spin the drey - dl, light the me-nor - ah, cel - e-brate this Ha - nuk-kah

ff

joy! _____

ff

joy! _____

He's Got the Whole World in His Hands

Black Spiritual

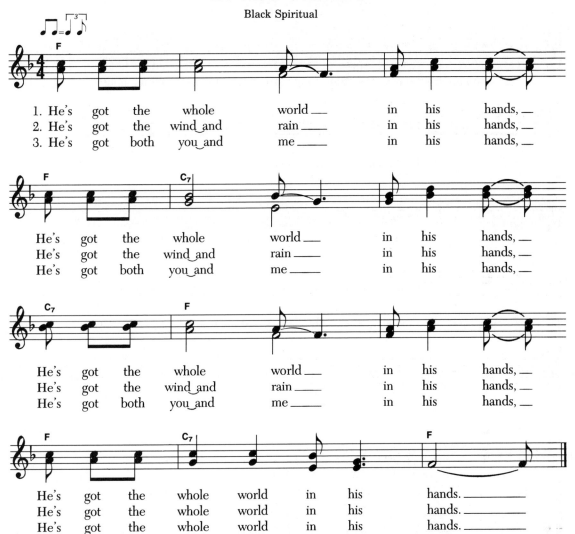

1. He's got the whole world ___ in his hands, ___
2. He's got the wind and rain ___ in his hands, ___
3. He's got both you and me ___ in his hands, ___

He's got the whole world ___ in his hands, ___
He's got the wind and rain ___ in his hands, ___
He's got both you and me ___ in his hands, ___

He's got the whole world ___ in his hands, ___
He's got the wind and rain ___ in his hands, ___
He's got both you and me ___ in his hands, ___

He's got the whole world in his hands. ___
He's got the whole world in his hands. ___
He's got the whole world in his hands. ___

Hosanna

Calypso Song from Jamaica

1. Ho-san-na, me build a house, _ oh, _ Ho-san-na, me build a house, _ oh, _ Ho-
2. Ho-san-na, me build a house, _ oh, _ Ho-san-na, me build a house, _ oh, _ Ho-

san-na, me build a house, _ oh, _ I built it on the sand-y ground. _
san-na, me build a house, _ oh, _ I build it on the sol-id ground. _

Me house built on _ a sand-y ground. _ It will fall, you see. Me
Me house built on _ a sol-id ground. _ It'll stand up, you see. Me

house built with sand all 'round. _ It will fall, you see.
house built on sol-id ground. _ It'll stand up, you see.

The rain _ will _ wet it up, Ha! Ha! The sun will burn it _ up, Ha! Ha! The
The rain _ can't _ wet it up, Ha! Ha! The sun can't burn it _ up, Ha! Ha! The

breeze will shake it _ up, Ha! Ha! The storm come blow it _ down, Ha! Ha! Me
breeze can't shake it _ up, Ha! Ha! The storm can't blow it _ down, Ha! Ha! Me

house can nev-er _ be, No! No! Me house too weak, you _ see, No! No! Me
house will ev-er _ be, Yes! Yes! Me house too strong, you _ see, Yes! Yes! Me

house will not stand, No! _ No! _ Storm blow it on-to the ground, Ha! Ha!
house will ever stand, Yes! _ Yes! _ Storm can't _ bring it to ground, Ha! Ha!

264

I Like It Here

Words and Music by Clay Boland

I like the U - nit - ed States of A - mer - i - ca, ____
I am so luck - y to be in A - mer - i - ca, ____

I like the way we all live with - out fear; ____
And I am thank - ful each day of the year, ____

I like to vote for my choice, ____ speak my mind, raise my voice,
For I can do as I please, ____ 'cause I'm free as the breeze,

1. Yes, I like it here. ____ **2.** like it here. ____

I'd like to climb to the top of a moun - tain so high, ____

Lift my head to the sky ____ and say how grate - ful am I ____

For the way that I'm liv - ing, I'm work - ing and giv - ing

And help - ing the land I hold dear, ____ Yes,

I like it, I like it, I like it here. ____

I Love Pasta

Words and Music by Sol Berkowitz

mac - a - ro - ni,   and tor - tel - li - ni,   and

ver - mi - cel - li,   and ra - vi - o - li,   and ri - ga - to -

ni, and fet - tu - cin - e,   ca - va - tel - li, man - i - cot - ti, per - ci - a -

tel - li,   can - ne - lo - ni,   di - ta - li - ni,   tag - li - a - tel - li,

mos - tac - cio - li,   cap - pel - let - ti,   and   zi - ti. _____

I Love the Mountains

Traditional

I love the moun - tains, I love the roll - ing hills,

I love the flow - ers, I love the daf - fo - dils,

I love the fire - side When all the lights are low,

Boom - de - ah - da, Boom - de - ah - da, Boom - de - ah - da, Boom - de - ah - da.

(Last time: Voice I sings the last phrase, "Boom-de-ah-da," etc. four times, Voice II sings this phrase three times, Voice III twice, Voice IV once, then all sing the Coda together.)

Boom did - dle - dee - dum - dum, Boom, boom.

If

Words and Music by David Gates

If a pic-ture paints a thou-sand words, then why can't I paint you?
man could be two plac-es at one time, I'd be with you;

The words will nev-er show the you I've come to know.
to-mor-row and to-day, be-side you all the way.

If a face could launch a thou-sand ships, then where am I to go?
If the world should stop re-volv-ing, spin-ning slow-ly down to die,

There's no one home but you. You're all that's left me,
I'd spend the end with you. And when the world was

too. And when my love for life is run-ning dry, you
through, then one by one the stars would all go out. Then

1. come and pour your-self on me. If a
you and I would

2. *rit.* sim-ply fly a-way.

Jolly Old Saint Nicholas

Traditional

1. Jol-ly old Saint Ni-cho-las, Lean your ear this way, Don't you tell a

sin-gle soul What I'm going to say; Christ-mas Eve is com-ing soon,

Now, you dear old man, Whis-per what you'll bring to me, Tell me if you can.

2. When the clock is striking twelve,
When I'm fast asleep,
Down the chimney tall and round,
With your pack you'll creep;
All the stockings you will find
Hanging in a row;
Mine will be the shortest one,
You'll be sure to know.

3. Johnny wants a pair of skates,
Susie wants a toy,
Nancy wants a story book,
One to bring her joy;
As for me, I'm not too sure,
So I'll say "goodnight,"
Choose for me, dear Santa Claus,
What you think is right.

Mangwani Mpulele

Zulu Folk Song   Adapted by Theodore Bikel

Mang - wa - ni mpu - le - le ki - nel - wa ki - tu - la (a mang-wa-ni)
mahng - wah-nee mpoo - lay-lay kee-nehl-wah kee-too - lah (ah mahng-wah-nee)

Mang - wa - ni mpu - le - le ki - nel - wa ki - tu - la. Le -
mahng - wah-nee mpoo - lay-lay kee-nehl-wah kee-too - lah lay -

hae-le mu-la,   le hae-le mu-le   ki-nel-wa ki-tu - la. (a mang-wa-ni) Le -
high-lay moo-lah   lay high-lay moo-lay   kee-nehl-wah kee-too - lah (ah mahng-wah-nee) lay-

hae-le mu-la,   le hae-le mu-le   ki-nel-wa ki-tu - la, a mang-wa-ni.
high-lay moo-lah   lay high-lay moo-lay   kee-nehl-wah kee-too - lah ah mahng-wah-nee

la. Mang - wa - ni mpu - le - le ki -nel -wa ki - tu -
lah mahng - wah-nee mpoo - lay-lay kee-nehl-wah kee-too -

la (a mang-wa-ni) Mang - wa - ni mpu - le - le ki -nel -wa ki -tu - la.
lah (ah mahng-wah-nee) mahng -wah-nee mpoo - lay-lay kee-nehl-wah kee-too - lah

Mary Ann

Calypso Song from the West Indies

All day, all night, Miss Ma - ry Ann, ____

Down by the sea - shore sift - ing sand, ____

Ev - en lit - tle child - ren join in the band, ____

Down by the sea - shore sift - ing sand. ____

2. All day, all night, Miss Mary Ann,
   Down by the seashore sifting sand,
   Young and old, come join the band,
   Down by the seashore sifting sand.

3. All day, all night, Miss Mary Ann,
   Down by the seashore sifting sand,
   Everybody come and join the band,
   Down by the seashore sifting sand.

The Mermaid

Traditional

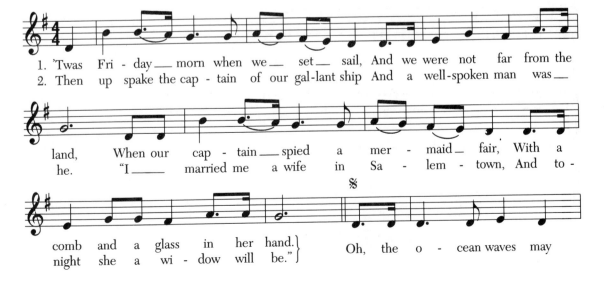

1. 'Twas Fri - day ____ morn when we ____ set ____ sail, And we were not far from the
2. Then up spake the cap - tain of our gal - lant ship And a well-spoken man was ____

land, When our cap - tain ____ spied a mer - maid ____ fair, With a
he. "I ____ married me a wife in Sa - lem - town, And to -

comb and a glass in her hand.⎫
night she a wi - dow will be."⎭   Oh, the o - cean waves may

roll, (let 'em roll) And the storm - y winds may blow, (let 'em blow,____) But

we poor sai - lors go skip-ping to the top, While the land - lub - bers lie down be -

Fine

low, (be - low, be - low,) while the land - lub - bers lie down be - low.

Slowly

3. Then three times a-round went our gal - lant____ ship, And three times a-round went

she (went she) Then three times a-round went our gal - lant____ ship, And she

sank to the bot - tom of the sea, _____ and she
(bot-tom of the sea)

D.S. al Fine

sank to the bot - tom of the sea.

A Mighty Fortress Is Our God

Melody by Martin Luther   Harmonization by J. S. Bach
Translation by Frederick H. Hedge

1. A might - y for - tress is____ our God, A bul - wark nev - er____
2. That word a - bove_ all earth - ly powers, No thanks to them, a -

fail - ing; Our help - er He _ a - mid _ the flood Of
bid - eth; The Spir - it and _ the gifts _ are ours Through

mor - tal ills pre - vail - ing: For still our an - cient foe Doth
Him who with us _ sid - eth: Let goods and kin - dred go, This

seek to work us woe; His craft and power are great, And,
mor - tal life al - so; The bod - y they may kill: God's

armed with cru - el hate, On earth is not his e - qual.
truth a - bid - eth still; His king - dom is for - ev - er.

Noble Dame

Words and Music by Manos Hadjidakis and Dorian Rudnytsky
Arranged by Larry Eisman

1. She was a la-dy, once a no-ble name, No-ble Dame, ___
2. She was a la-dy, once with-out a care, gold-en hair ___

She had a sil-ver ring from the king; ___
She was the on-ly friend of the king; ___

Give her a nick-el, take her out to dine, out ___ to dine ___
May-be she'll come and ask you for your name, no-ble dame, ___

Com-fort her if she sighs and then cries. ___
We'll give our love to her on her way. ___

Look for her by the foun-tain on the road, ___ say, ___ "Hel-

lo," ___ Don't be a-fraid to smile and then go.

And if you see her talk-ing to her-self ___ all ___ a-

lone, ___ Leave her a-lone her heart is at home.

278

One Tin Soldier

Words and Music by Dennis Lambert and Brian Potter

1. Lis-ten, chil-dren, to a sto-ry that was writ-ten long a-go,
2. So the peo-ple of the val-ley sent a mes-sage up the hill
3. Now the val-ley cried with an-ger, "Mount your hors-es! Draw your sword!"

'Bout a king-dom on a moun-tain and the val-ley folk be-low;
Ask-ing for the bur-ied treas-ure, tons of gold for which they'd kill.
And they killed the moun-tain peo-ple so they won their just re-ward.

On the moun-tain was a trea-sure bur-ied deep be-neath a stone,
Came an an-swer from the king-dom "with our broth-ers we will share
Now they stood be-side the treas-ure on the moun-tain, dark and red

And the val-ley peo-ple swore they'd have it for their ver-y
All the se-crets of our moun-tain, all the rich-es bur-ied
Turned the stone and looked be-neath it, "Peace on earth" was all it

own.
there." Go a-head and hate your neigh-bor, go a-head and cheat a friend.
said.

Do it in the name of heav-en, jus-ti-fy it in the end.

There won't be an-y trum-pets blow-in' come the judg-ment day;

On the blood-y morn-ing af-ter one tin sol-dier rides a-way.

Puttin' on the Style ⑬

American Folk Song   New Words and New Music Adaptation by Norman Cazden

REFRAIN

Put-tin' on the ag-o-ny, put-tin' on the style, That's what all the young folks are do-in' all the while. And as I look a-round me, I'm ver-y apt to smile To see so man-y peo-ple put-tin' on the style.

VERSE

1. Young man in a car-riage,___ driv-in' like ___ he's mad, With a pair of hors-es___ he bor-rowed from his dad; He cracks his whip so live-ly just to watch his la-dy smile,___ But she knows he's on-ly put-tin' on the style.

2. Sweet six-teen and goes to school just___ to see the boys, Turns and laughs and gig-gles___ at ev-'ry lit-tle noise; She turns this way a lit-tle, then___ turns that way a-while, But we know that she's on-ly put-tin' on the style.

3. Young man home from col-lege___ makes__ a great dis-play, With a fan-cy ad-jec-tive that he can hard-ly say; It can't be found in Web-ster's, and it won't be for a-while, But ev-'ry-bod-y knows_ he's put-tin' on the style.

Raisins and Almonds

Yiddish Words and Music by Abraham Goldfaden   English Words by David ben Avraham

Freely

In dem beys ha-mik-dosh, in a vin-kl chey-der, zitst di al-
ihn dehm bays hah-mihk-dohsh ihn a veen-k(uh)l khay-dehr zihtst dee ahl-
In midst of the vil-lage, there's a tem-ple so love-ly, In-side the

mo-ne, bas Tzi-on a-leyn. Ir ben yo-chi-dl, yi-de-len,
maw-nuh bahs tsee-awhn ah-layn eer behn yoh-chee-d(uh)l yee-duh-lehn
door sits a wi-dow a-lone. In the cra-dle she rocks lies her

vigt zi ki-sey-der, un zingt im tzum shlo-fn a li-de-le
vihgt zee kee-say-dehr oon zeenkt ihm tsoom shluh-f(oh)n a lih-duh-luh
ba-by a sleep-ing, and she lulls him to sleep with a sweet slum-ber

sheyn. "Un-ter yi-de-les vi-ge-le_____ shteyt a klor veys
shayn oon-tehr yee-duh-luhs vee-guh-luh shtayt a klawr vays
song. "Neath the cra-dle that holds__ your_ dream,__ stands a goat as

tsi-ge-le._____ Dos tsi-ge-le iz ge-fo-rn hand-len.__
tsee-guh-luh duhs tsee-guh-luh ihz guh-faw-r(uh)n hahnt-lehn
white__ as__ cream.__ The goat__ will be__ soon__ to mar-ket.__

__ Dos vet zayn dayn ba-ruf._____ ro-zhin-kes__ mit
duhs veht zayn dayn bah-roof roh-zheen-kuhs miht
__ There a prom-ise to keep:_____ To buy you rais-ins and

mand-len._____ Shlof-zhe, yi-de-le, shlof."_____
mund-l(eh)n shluhf-zhuh yee-duh-luh shluhf
al-monds._____ Sleep, my lit-tle one, sleep."_____

© 1961 Ethnic Publishing Corp. Hasbrouck Heights, N.J. International copyright secured. Used by permission.

Sakura

(Cherry Blossoms)

Japanese Folk Song   Arranged by Bruce Saylor

ranged a - gainst the lim - pid __ sky; Mist - like pe - tals,

hues be - lie; but these clouds ex - ude per - fume.

Come with me, Come with me, see the sweet cher - ries in

Come with me, Come with me, see the trees in

bloom. _____ Sa - ku - ra, Sa - ku -

bloom. _____ Sa - ku - ra, Sa - ku - ra,

ra _____ Sa -

ya yo i no so ra - wa, mi - wa - ta - su

- ku - ra ka - su mi ka ku - mu - ka,

ka - gi - ri, ka - su mi ka ku - mu - ka

f espr.   *poco rit.*   *p dolce*

ni o i ___ zo ___ i zu - ru. ___ Come with me,

f espr.   *p dolce*

ni o i zo i zu - ru. Come with me,

sempre dim.   *pp*

Come with me, see the sweet cher - ries in bloom. ___

sempre dim.   *pp*

Come with me, see the sweet ___ trees in bloom. ___

Scattin' with Solfège

Sol Berkowitz   Based on a Violin Study by Kreutzer

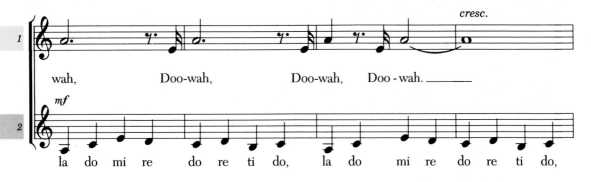

Sentimental Journey

Words and Music by Bud Green, Les Brown and Ben Homer

Gon - na take a sen - ti - men - tal jour - ney, Gon - na set my
Got my bag, I got my res - er - va - tion, Spent each dime I

heart at ease.__ Gon - na make a sen - ti - men - tal jour - ney, To re - new old
could af - ford.__ Like a child in wild an - ti - ci - pa - tion, Long to hear that

mem - o - ries.__ Sev - en, __ that's the time we leave, at sev - en. __
"All __ a - board." __

I'll be wait - in' up for Heav - en, __ Count - in' ev - 'ry mile of

rail - road track _ that takes me back. _ Nev - er thought my heart could be so "yearn - y."

Why did I de - cide to roam? _ Got - ta take this

sen - ti - men - tal jour - ney, sen - ti - men - tal jour - ney home. _

So My Sheep May Safely Graze

Words and Music by Rod McKuen

1. So my sheep may safe - ly graze _ I'd climb the high - est hill, ____ And
2. All good shep - herds watch their flocks _ to the low - est lamb ____
3. Last night there were sol - diers on _ the road ____ be - low the town ____ And

keep a watch ____ out for the hawk _ and for the howl - ing wolf. ____ I
So that they ____ may safe - ly graze _ and nev - er come to harm. ____
crea - tures _ in the heav - ens with _ wings ____ of shin - y gold. ____

made a friend out of the wind _ and got to know the snow. So
Guard - ed from the hunt - er's horn _ shield - ed from the sun.
One of them came close to me _ say - ing, "Do not be a - fraid. A

e - ven in the win - ter - time _ my sheep may safe - ly graze. ____
All my sheep may safe - ly graze _ in far fields or at home. ____ Call - ing,
child of God was born this night; _ Your sheep may safe - ly graze." ____

REFRAIN

"Come, sheep, come, I'll count you one by one. One for John and one for Ja - cob,

"Come, sheep, come, I'll count you one by one. Ah _____

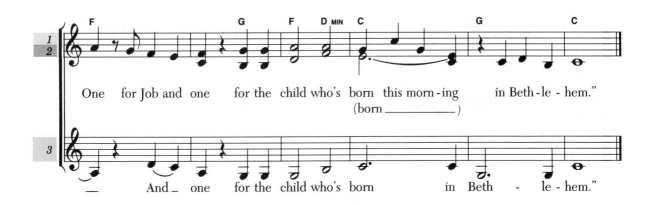

One for Job and one for the child who's born this morn-ing in Beth-le - hem."
(born _____)

And _ one for the child who's born in Beth - le - hem."

Spring Song

English Words by Theron Haithwaite   Music by Franz Joseph Haydn

mp
The ear - ly spring-time breez - es blow - ing, Re -

fresh - ing ev - 'ry field and glade. _ To all the breath of life be -

stow - ing, The fra-grance in the cool-ing shade. _ We

won - der in the gift of spring - time, We cel - e-brate the length-'ning

mf
days. We sing _ the _ song of earth's re - new - ing, And

mp *rit.*   *a tempo*   *rit.*
hymn our _ grate-ful spi-rits' praise. We hymn our grate-ful spi-rits' praise.

The Star-Spangled Banner

Words by Francis Scott Key   Music by John Stafford Smith

1. Oh, ___ say! can you see by the dawn's ear - ly light,

What so proud - ly we hailed at the twi - light's last gleam - ing,

Whose broad stripes and bright stars, through the per - il - ous fight,

O'er the ram - parts we watched were so gal - lant - ly stream - ing?

And the rock - ets' red glare, the bombs burst - ing in air,

Gave proof through the night that our flag was still there.

Oh, say, does that ___ Star - Span - gled Ban - ner ___ yet ___ wave ___

O'er the land___ of the free and the home of the brave.

2. On the shore, dimly seen through the mists of the deep,
   Where the foe's haughty host in dread silence reposes,
   What is that which the breeze, o'er the towering steep,
   As it fitfully blows, half conceals, half discloses?
   Now it catches the gleam of the morning's first beam,
   In full glory reflected now shines on the stream;
   'Tis the Star-Spangled Banner, oh, long may it wave
   O'er the land of the free and the home of the brave!

3. Oh, thus be it ever when free men shall stand
   Between their loved homes and the war's desolation!
   Blest with vict'ry and peace, may the heav'n-rescued land
   Praise the Pow'r that hath made and preserved us a nation!
   Then conquer we must, for our cause it is just,
   And this be our motto: "In God is our trust!"
   And the Star-Spangled Banner in triumph shall wave
   O'er the land of the free and the home of the brave!

Step to the Rear 🔴14

from *How Now, Dow Jones*

Words by Carolyn Leigh   Music by Elmer Bernstein

Will ev - 'ry one here ___ kind - ly step to the rear ___ And let a win - ner lead the way; ___ Here's where we sep - a - rate the notes from the noise, ___ The men from the boys, ___ the rose from the poi - son i - vy.

Back in the bunch, ___ I came up with a hunch, ___ This was an

up and at 'em day; _____ It's one of those spells _

___ when you hear the right bells ___ And your hor - o-scope tells _

___ you to say. _____ Will ev - 'ry - one here _

___ kind - ly step to the rear ___ And let a win - ner

lead the way! _____ I hear those trum - pets

be - gin to blare, _____ And now I'm Wash - ing -

ton up - on the Del - a - ware. Will

Countermelody

Here he comes and things are

Melody

ev - 'ry - one here _____ kind - ly step to the rear ___

thumbs up, Fol - low the lead - er

— And let a win - ner lead the

all down the way; Here he comes, a

way; _____ Here's where we sep - a - rate the

hick of a fel - ler, But fol - ler his smell -

duck from the quack, ___ The ace from the pack, ___

- er I'd say, "O - kay!"

_____ The pip from the mack - in - tosh - es.

There he goes and boy, it

Back in the group, ___ I came up with the scoop. _

shows ya, Up on your toes ya

_ This was the time to rise and

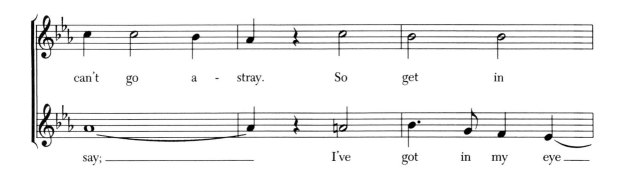

can't go a - stray. So get in

say; _ I've got in my eye _

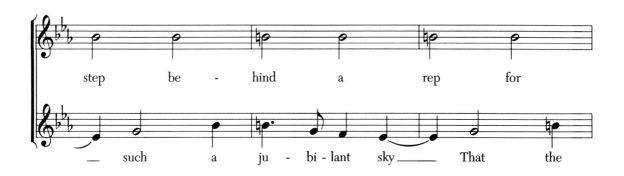

step be - hind a rep for

_ such a ju - bi - lant sky _ That the

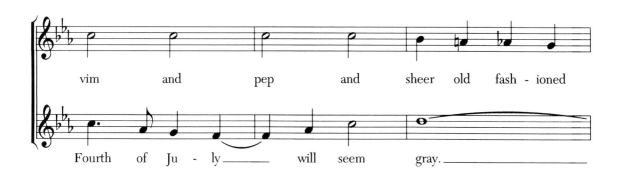

vim and pep and sheer old fash - ioned

Fourth of Ju - ly _ will seem gray. _

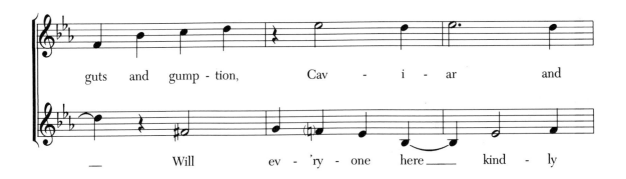

guts and gump - tion, Cav - i - ar and

Will ev - 'ry - one here kind - ly

pheas - ant for din - ner, A win - ner will lead the

step to the rear. And let a win - ner lead the

way, Just let a win - ner, let a win - ner, let a

way, Just let a win - ner

cool and crow - ing win - ner lead the way.

lead the way.

Thanksgiving Calypso

Words and Music by David Eddleman

1. Once a year __ we set a - side a day __ for cel - e - brat - ing in a
2. Say a thank - you for the air we breathe, __ the rain - y days __ a - mak - ing

spe - cial way, __ To count our bless - ings, count 'em by the score: the
shin - y leaves; __ The sun a - beam - ing on the gar - den wall __ is say - ing,

things we have __ to be thank - ful for. __ Let's sing a song of grat - i -
"Hap - py Thanks - giv - ing" to one and all. __

tude, Let's sing a song of hap - py days; We'll sing a thank - you song to

you, We'll sing a song of joy and praise. _____

Say, "Thank - you" for the fields __ of grain, say, "Thank - you" for the fall - ing rain,

Say, "Thank - you" for the chance __ to live in peace and har - mo - ny. _____

Time in a Bottle

Words and Music by Jim Croce

Tina Singu

Folk Song from Africa

Ti - na Sing - u, le - lu - vu - tae - o. Wat - sha, Wat - sha, Wat - sha.
tee - nah sing - oo lee - loo - voo - tye - oh waht - shah waht - shah waht - shah
We are burn - ing, burn - ing the fire; _____ burn - ing, _ burn - ing, _ burn - ing.

Wat - sha, _ Wat - sha, _ Wat - sha, _ Wat - sha, _ Wat - sha.
waht - shah waht - shah waht - shah waht - shah waht - shah
Burn - ing, _ burn - ing, _ burn - ing, _ burn - ing, _ burn - ing.

La, la la la la la la, la la la la la la, la la la la la la la la la la.

Try to Remember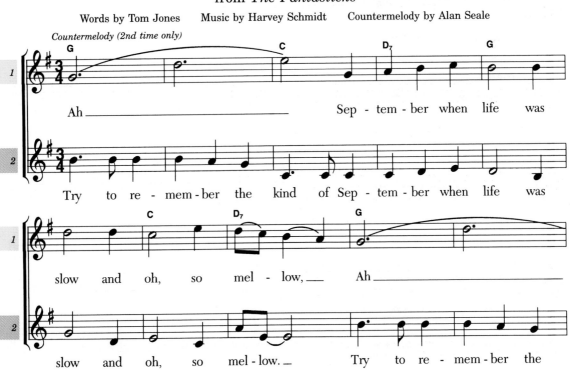

from *The Fantasticks*

Words by Tom Jones   Music by Harvey Schmidt   Countermelody by Alan Seale

Countermelody (2nd time only)

1: Ah _____ Sep - tem - ber when life was

2: Try to re - mem - ber the kind of Sep - tem - ber when life was

1: slow and oh, so mel - low, _ Ah _____

2: slow and oh, so mel - low. _ Try to re - mem - ber the

Wi Yo He Yo

American Indian Song

Transcribed from the Library of Congress recording AFSL36.

You've Got a Friend

Words and Music by Carole King

When you're down ___ and trou - bled, And you need ___ some love and care, ___
 ___ a - bove ___ you grows ___ dark ___ and full of clouds, _

 ___ And noth - in' ___ noth - in' is go - in' right, ___
 ___ And that ol' ___ north wind be - gins _ to blow, ___

Close your eyes _ and think of me, _ And soon I ___ will be there ___ To
Keep your head _ to - geth - er, ___ and call my _ name out loud; ___

bright - en up ___ e - ven your dark - est night. ___
Soon you'll hear _ me ___ knock - in' at ___ your door. ___ You just call _

 ___ out my ___ name, ___ and you know ___ wher - ev - er I am, _

 ___ I'll come run - nin' ___ to see you a - gain. ___

Win - ter, spring, sum - mer or fall, ___ All you have to do is call, ___

and I'll be there. You've got a friend.

If the sky there. Now

ain't it good to know that you've got a friend, when peo-ple can be so cold?

They'll hurt you, yes, and de-sert you, and take your soul if you

D.S. al Coda

let them. Oh, but don't you let them. You just call

Coda

there yes, I will, You've got a friend. You've got a

Repeat and fade

friend. It's so good to know you've got a

Glossary

a cappella (p. 72) A term used to indicate unaccompanied choral singing; "in chapel style."

accent (p. 23) A single tone or chord louder than those around it (>).

acoustical (acoustics) (p. 146) Pertaining to the physical properties of sound: frequency (pitch), amplitude (loudness), overtone structure (tone color) and duration (length).

bar line (p. 116) The vertical line on the staff, used to mark off groupings of beats.

beat (p. 15) A repeating pulse that can be felt in some music.

chorale (p. 29) A homophonic harmonization of a hymn tune. *See* homophony.

chord (p. 42) Three or more different tones played or sung together.

compound meter (p. 153) A grouping of beats in which three beats are felt as one.

concerto (p. 25) Piece for a solo instrument with orchestra, usually in three movements.

diction (p. 83) The pronunciation and enunciation of words in singing.

dissonance (p. 37) Interval or chord that sounds unstable, and pulls towards a consonance.

duet (p. 185) Any two-part composition written for two performers.

ensemble (p. 197) A group of players or singers.

finale (p. 64) [fee NAH leh] Last movement of a composition, such as a symphony or concerto.

folk song (p. 53) Song of unknown authorship which has for generations been current among the people of a nation or region.

form (p. 29) The structure of a composition; the way its musical materials are organized.

fret (p. 101) A strip of metal across the fingerboard of a guitar or similar instrument. The player raises or lowers the pitch by pressing a string into contact with a fret.

fugue (p. 133) A musical form based on imitation, in which the main melody (subject) and related melodies (countersubjects) are varied in different ways. The texture is polyphonic. *See* polyphonic texture.

graphic notation (p. 57) Notation using a picture to represent sounds (rather than using traditional notation for exact pitches).

Gregorian chant (p. 70) *See* plainsong.

harmony (p. 42) A related succession of chords.

homophonic texture (p. 25) A melodic line supported by a harmonic accompaniment.

improvisation (p. 17) The art of making up the music as the performer goes along.

interval (p. 108) The distance from one tone to another. The smallest interval in traditional Western music is the half step (f-f♯, f♯-g, etc.). Contemporary music often uses smaller intervals, as does music of other cultures.

jazz (p. 15) A style that grew out of the music of black Americans, then took many different substyles: ragtime, blues, cool jazz, swing, bebop, rock, etc. It features solo improvisations over a set harmonic progression.

key (p. 42) The particular scale on which a piece of music or a section of it is based, named for its tonic or key-tone or "home-base" tone. (The key of D major indicates that the major scale starting and ending on the tone D is being used.)

key signature (p. 103) An indication of key consisting of sharps or flats placed on the staff at the beginning of a composition.

major (p. 102) Tonally, a key that is based on a major scale—a scale that contains a step-pattern of whole, whole, half, whole, whole, whole, half.

medley (p. 30) A set of songs grouped together and sung without interruption.

melody (p. 25) A succession of single tones with rhythm, forming a recognizable musical idea.

meter (p. 36) The way beats of music are grouped, often in sets of two or in sets of three. The meter signature, or time signature (e.g., $\frac{3}{4}$, $\frac{2}{4}$), tells how many beats are in the group, or measure (top number), and the kind of note that gets one beat (bottom number).

metronome (p. 129) A mechanical or electronic device that indicates precise tempo markings.

minor (p. 104) Tonally, a key that is based on a minor scale—a scale that contains a step-pattern of whole, half, whole, whole, half, whole, whole.

monophonic texture (p. 73) A single unaccompanied melody line.

monophony (p. 73) The musical texture consisting of a single unaccompanied melody line.

motive (p. 111) A short musical fragment.

multimeter (p. 120) Changing from one meter to another in successive measures.

neume (p. 70) Plainchant notation—originally slanted lines indicating the rise and fall of the melody. Later, various-shaped noteheads that rested on a four- or five-line staff.

notation (p. 70) Symbols that represent specific pitches and durations in music.

opera (p. 82) A theatrical production combining drama, vocal and orchestral music, costumes, scenery, and sometimes dance.

oratorio (p. 82) A musical drama for voices and orchestra, often based on a religious narrative; usually performed without scenery or action.

ostinato (p. 145) A musical idea that repeats throughout a piece or a section of a piece.

pentatonic (p. 106) Music based on a five-tone scale. A common pentatonic scale corresponds to tones 1, 2, 3, 5, and 6 of the major scale.

phrase (p. 41) A melodic idea that acts as a complete thought, something like a sentence.

pitch (p. 36) The highness or lowness of a tone.

plainchant (p. 70) *See* plainsong.

plainsong (p. 70) Monophonic chant sung usually with even rhythm on Latin texts. Plainsong is one of the earliest examples of notated music. *See* monophony.

polyphony (p. 73) Music consisting of two or more independent melodic lines sounding together.

polyphonic texture (p. 78) Two or more independent melody lines sounding together.

polyrhythm (p. 9) Several different rhythm patterns going on at the same time, often resulting in conflicts of meter.

rhythm (p. 9) The combination of sounds and silences in the same or differing lengths.

riff (p. 18) A term used in jazz for a repeated, short, strongly rhythmic phrase. *See* ostinato.

rondo (p. 174) A form in which the A section alternates with two contrasting sections, creating a plan of ABACA.

round (p. 50) A form in which a melody begins in one part and then is continually and exactly repeated by other parts in an overlapping fashion.

scale (p. 42) An arrangement of pitches from lower to higher according to a specific pattern of intervals. Major, minor, pentatonic, whole-tone, and chromatic are five kinds of scales. Each one has its own arrangement of pitches.

score (p. 60) The musical notation of a composition, showing all vocal and instrumental parts.

sequence (p. 111) The repetition of a melody pattern at a higher or lower pitch level.

sprechstimme (p. 56) A vocal style somewhere between singing and speaking, used mainly by composers of atonal music.

staff (p. 43) A set of five equally spaced horizontal lines on which musical notes are written.

style (p. 24) In music, style refers to the way in which melody, rhythm, and harmony create a special "sound."

syncopation (p. 20) An arrangement of rhythm in which prominent or important tones begin on weak beats or weak parts of beats, giving a catchy, "off-balance" movement to the music.

tempo (p. 128) The speed of the beat.

theme (p. 17) An important melody that occurs several times in a piece of music.

tone cluster (p. 66) A group of tones lying no more than a step apart and produced, often on the piano, by pressing down on a section of the keyboard with the fist, forearm, or a board.

tone color (p. 27) The special sound of an instrument or voice.

triad (p. 42) A chord of three tones, usually built in thirds—an interval of a third on top of another interval of a third.

trio (p. 185) Any three-part composition written for three performers.

triplet (p. 124) A rhythm pattern made by playing three equal sounds in the space of two of the same value.

variation (p. 112) Music that changes a theme in some important ways.

wave forms (p. 68) Basic electronic tone colors produced by an oscillator. Each waveform has a name that describes the way it looks when seen on an oscilloscope.

Can You Read This?

Can You Read This?

You can read the words in a traffic sign because you have learned that certain letters represent certain sounds.

You can begin to read music as you learn which musical symbols represent which musical sounds.

Musical symbols can represent the rhythm of music. A series of notes that are the same represents an even rhythm pattern. For example, you can clap this steady quarter-note rhythm:

Combining symbols for longer and shorter sounds will make a more interesting rhythm. Clap this pattern:

Clap this more complicated rhythm pattern:

All of the patterns in "Can You Read This?" can be performed with a song in your book.

Add the musical staff and you can read the direction of the melody, up and down, along with the rhythm.

This simple *ostinato* melody moves up and then down. It always moves by *step*. Each note is just next door to the note before it.

This ostinato moves *by leap*. A leap jumps over the note next to it and moves to one that is further away.

This melody has an interesting pattern with a *dotted note*. Clap the ♪ pattern in groups of six:

6/8 meter also falls into a pattern of two. Each *measure* will have two dotted quarter notes. Clap the even pattern of two ♩.

Clap the even pattern of
dotted quarter notes: 6/8 ♩. ♩. | ♩. ♩. :||

Take the dots off the quarter
notes, and add an eighth note: 6/8 ♩ ♪♩ ♪|♩ ♪♩ ♪:||

This melody uses all three of these 6/8 meter patterns. The melody moves mostly by step.

Reference Bank   309

Here is a longer melody. It will be easier to sing if you look for
repeated patterns.

Here are two melodies that can be sung with the same song. The
first one is quite simple.

Now try this more complicated melody. There are patterns that
repeat on different pitches. These repeating patterns are called
sequences.

Here are two melodies in minor tonality.

This melody will work with a song in your book. Be careful to observe the repeat pattern, or it will not fit!

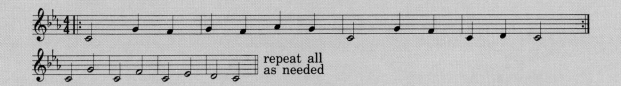

Sometimes this melody moves by step, and sometimes it leaps. The patterns are sometimes similar, but no two patterns are exactly alike. Patterns that are identical are easier to sing. However, variations in the pattern make the music more interesting.

Here is a melody in a major key. It begins with easy, even step-wise patterns, and then changes to skips and dotted patterns. Notice the meter changes!

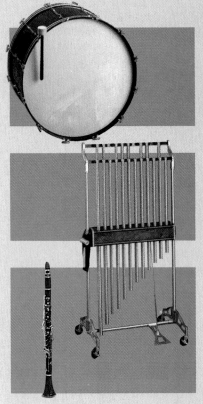

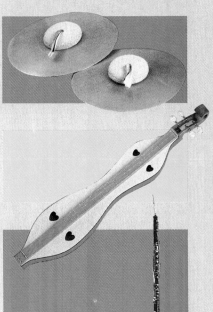

Bass Drum   A large, cylinder-shaped, metal drum with two "heads" made of stretched calfskin or plastic. The drum rests on its metal side and the player stands behind it, beating either side with a large, padded mallet.
• The bass drum is often used for dramatic effect in the orchestra. It can produce a deep booming roar or a soft, thudding heartbeat. (p. 141)

Chimes   A set of eighteen long, metal tubes (usually brass), suspended from a tall frame. The player stands beside them and strikes the top of the tubes with a wooden hammer.
• Chimes ring with a hollow, metallic tone and are frequently used to imitate church bells. (p. 140)

Clarinet   A cylinder-shaped wind instrument, usually wooden but sometimes metal or synthetic, with a single reed in the mouthpiece. The player blows into the mouthpiece to make the sound and changes the pitch by pressing keys on the side of the instrument.
• The clarinet has three "voices." In the lower register it is soft and hollow-sounding. The middle register is clear and bright, and the highest notes are more intense and can be very piercing. (p. 17)

Cymbals   Two shallow, metal plates, usually made of brass, fitted with leather hand-straps. One is held in each hand and they are clapped together to produce the sound.
• Cymbals vary in size. While large ones make an earth-shattering crash, small cymbals may be played for a light, delicate, rhythmic accompaniment. (p. 202)

Dulcimer   A stringed folk instrument usually played by plucking. It has a long thin body that is usually made of pine or maple.
• The sound of the dulcimer is soft and has a haunting, "faraway" quality.

English Horn   A wooden instrument shaped like a cylinder with a bulb-shaped bell at the bottom. It has a double reed which the player blows into to make the sound. Keys on the side of the instrument are pressed to change the pitch.
• The sound of the English horn is similar to the exotic "oriental" tone color of the oboe, but its "voice" is lower and the tone is richer and warmer. (p. 141)

Flute A small metal instrument shaped like a round piece of pipe. The player blows across an open mouthpiece in the side of the flute near one end, and presses button-like keys to change pitches. Originally flutes were made of wood, but most are now metal, some even gold or silver.
• The sound of the flute is pure, clear, and sweet. The lower notes are very soft and gentle; the higher register is brighter and louder. (p. 62)

French Horn A medium-sized brass instrument made of coiled tubing, with a large bell at the end. The player sits with the horn held down near his lap, and keeps one hand in the bell to control the pitch and tone. He *buzzes* his lips against the mouthpiece to make the sound. The pitch is changed by pressing valves in the side of the horn.
• The sound of the French horn is mellow and warm, and not as loud or assertive as the other brass instruments. (p. 141)

Gong A broad, concave metal disc, usually made of brass and hung vertically in a frame. The player strikes the gong slightly off-center with a soft-headed mallet.
• A sensitive player can evoke loud or soft, short or long tones from the gong, which reverberate with a rich, shimmering sound. (p. 140)

Oboe A small, wooden, cylinder-shaped wind instrument. The player blows into a double reed to make the sound, and changes pitch by pressing keys on the side of the instrument.
• The sound of the oboe is thin and sweet, often sounding exotic or melancholy. Unlike many other woodwind instruments, the sound gets sweeter and softer as it goes higher. (p. 141)

Recorder A simple wooden flute dating back to the Middle Ages. It is sounded by blowing into a "whistle" mouthpiece at one end. Holes in the side of the recorder are covered and uncovered to change the pitches.
• The recorder has a delicate, quiet tone, even in its more piercing higher register. The recorder comes in many sizes, the larger ones sounding lower, the smaller ones higher. (p. 134)

Saxophone A woodwind instrument invented by Adolphe Sax in the nineteenth century by placing a clarinet type reed mouthpiece on a piece of brass tubing.
• The saxophone has a warm, brassy-but-mellow sound that makes it ideal in jazz ensembles. (p. 17)

Snare Drum   A small, cylinder-shaped drum. Two heads made of calfskin or plastic are stretched over the metal shell and strings wrapped in wire ("snares") are fixed to the bottom. When the player strikes the top with sticks, the snares vibrate in response.
• A sharp, steady, rhythmic accompaniment is often played on the snare drum. It can also produce a long, raspy, rolling sound. (p. 140)

String Bass   A large wooden string instrument which is either bowed or plucked. The string bass is taller than most players, who must stand up or sit on a tall stool to play it.
• The sound of the string bass is very dark and resonant, particularly in the lower notes. The plucked notes are very useful for establishing a strong "beat," both in classical music and popular music. (p. 17)

Tambourine   A small, shallow drum with one head and a wooden shell. Circular metal disks ("jingles") hang loosely in pairs around the circumference of the shell. The player holds the tambourine in one hand and shakes it or strikes it with the other hand or on the hip.
• A shimmery, metallic sound rattles from the tambourine. (p. 141)

Timpani   A set of two or more large, basin-shaped drums made of copper or brass, with calfskin or plastic stretched over the top. Each drum has a different pitch, which can be adjusted by means of a pedal at the base. Usually only one player is in charge of all four drums and plays them by striking the top with two mallets.
• The timpani are the most important percussion instruments, for they provide strong rhythmic and tonal support to the orchestra. The usually produce a deep, insistent rumbling but can also punch out sharp, loud notes. (p. 23)

Trombone   A fairly large brass instrument with a large bell at the end of the tubing. The sound is made by *buzzing* the lips against the mouthpiece. The pitches are changed by pushing and pulling a metal "slide," lengthening and shortening the tubing.
• The trombone can sound very aggressive and noisy; but in its softer "voice" it can be warm and mellow. (p. 202)

Vibraphone   A xylophone-like instrument with metal bars. An electronic device creates a slow or fast vibrato, giving the instrument its name.
• The vibraphone has a mellow, "sweet" sound, especially when the "vibrato device" is engaged. (p. 17)

Xylophone   A melodic percussion instrument with a keyboard of wooden bars and played with mallets.
• The xylophone has a bright, brittle sound that makes it effective in percussive or humorous passages. (p. 17)

Classified Index

FOLK AND TRADITIONAL SONGS

Africa
Mangwani Mpulele 272
Tina Singu 301

American Indian
Wi Yo He Yo 303

Black America
He's Got the Whole World in His Hands 263
Nine Hundred Miles 7
On My Journey 170
This Old Hammer 148
When the Saints Go Marching In 196

British Isles
Hunter, The 78
King of Love My Shepherd Is, The 79
Men of Harlech 95
Merry Minstrels 103
Oh, Dear! What Can the Matter Be? 11
We're All Together Again 80

Chile
Mi caballo blanco 118
My White Horse 118

Cuba
Elegua 13

Hispanic
Con el vito (Spain) 154
De colores (Mexico) 130
Elegua (Cuba) 13
Laredo (Mexico) 186
Mi caballo blanco 118
My White Horse 118

Israel, Hebrew, Jewish
Dodi Li 175
Gilu Hagalilim 200, 201, 202
Glee Reigns in Galilee 200, 201, 202
Hatikvah 104
Raisins and Almonds 281
Tumbalalaika (arrangement) 120

Japan
Sakura 282

Mexico
De colores 130
Laredo 186

Spain
Con el vito 154

United States
Erie Canal 258
I Love the Mountains 269
I Ride an Old Paint (medley) 30
Mermaid, The 275
Old Hundred 72
Puttin' on the Style 280
Red River Valley (medley) 30
Row, Row, Row Your Boat 113
Streets of Laredo (medley) 30

West Indies
Hosanna 264
Mary Ann 275
Water Come a Me Eye 84

HOLIDAY, SEASONAL, AND SPECIAL-OCCASION SONGS

Patriotic
America 257
America the Beautiful 166
Chester 34
I Like It Here 265
Marine's Hymn, The 99, 173
Star-Spangled Banner, The 292
This Land Is Your Land 114

Spring
De colores 130
Sakura 282
Spring Song 291
While Strolling Through the Park 81

Thanksgiving
America 257
America the Beautiful 166
King of Love My Shepherd Is, The 79
Old Hundred 72
Thanksgiving Calypso 298

Valentine's Day
Hello, My Baby 100
Let It Snow 204
Tell Me Why 132
Where Is Love? 222
You Are My Sunshine 21
You've Got a Friend 304

Winter Holidays
Here We Come A-Singing 260
Jolly Old St. Nicholas 271
Let It Snow 204
So My Sheep May Safely Graze 290

LISTENING LIBRARY

The following selections are heard in their entirety.

Alford: *Colonel Bogey March* 174
Anderson: *Belle of the Ball* 118
Applegate: *Coney Island Baby* 189
Bach: *Fugue in D Minor* 133
Bach: *Minuet* 170
Barber: *Adagio for Strings* 140
Bart: *Oliver!* selections 216
Bartók: *Mikrokosmos*, "Wrestling" 66
Beethoven: *Egmont Overture* (Call Chart 4) 51
Beethoven: *Für Elise* (Call Chart 8) 175
Beethoven: *Minuet in G* 66
Black Spiritual: *Swing Low, Sweet Chariot* 187
Britten: *Young Person's Guide to the Orchestra*, "Introduction" 207
Brubeck: *Unsquare Dance* 157
Chopin: *Waltz in C♯ Minor* (three performances) 139
Ciani: *Composition for Synthesizer* 164
Davis: *You Are My Sunshine* (jazz version) 21
Eddleman: *Autoharp Fantasy* 59
Eddleman: *Brass Quartet* "In Honorem Paul Hindemith," Movement 1 140
Eddleman: *Tales from the Latin Woods* 141
Eisman: *Do the Mambo* 145
Ellington: *Dooji-Wooji* 144
Faini: *Afro-Amero* (Call Chart 2) 23
Foster-Brubeck: *Camptown Races* (jazz arrangement) 198
Glass: *The Photographer*, "A Gentleman's Honor" 199
Glière: *Russian Sailors' Dance* 141
Goodman-Christian: *Seven Come Eleven* (Call Chart 1) 17
Goodman-Christian: *Seven Come Eleven* (without call numbers) 19
Gottschalk: *Pasquinade* 125
Grieg: *Peer Gynt*, "In the Hall of the Mountain King" 149
Handel: *Judas Maccabaeus*, "Hallelujah, Amen" 82
Haydn: *St. Anthony Chorale* 29
Holst: *The Planets*, "Mercury" 69
Joplin: *The Entertainer* 125
LeCaine: *Dripsody* 58
Lennon and McCartney: *The Long and Winding Road* 139
Lewis: *The Golden Striker*, "No Sun in Venice" 197

Liszt: *Concert Etude No. 3 in D♭ Major* ("Un Sospiro") 52
Lotti: *Kyrie* 74
Massenet: *Le Cid*, "Aragonaise" 208
McDaniels: *River* 147
Milhaud: *La cheminée du Roi René*, Movement 1 140
Mozart: *Symphony No. 40 in G Minor*, Movement 3 36
Oh Dear, What Can the Matter Be? with rhythm complex 12
Penderecki: *Threnody for the Victims of Hiroshima* 67
Prince and Ray: *Boogie-Woogie Bugle Boy* 186
Prokofiev: *Classical Symphony*, Movement 3, "Gavotte" 60
Raaijmakers: *Contrasts*, Part 2 (Call Chart 5) 69
Read: *The Aztec Gods*, Movement 1 140
Santana: *Gitano* 13
Schoenberg: *Pierrot lunaire*, "The Dandy" 56
Seeger: *Where Have All the Flowers Gone?* 29
Shostakovich: *Symphony No. 1 in F*, Movement 2 36
Smaldone: *Piece for Synthesizer* 146
Sondheim: *Send in the Clowns* (two performances) 138
Stravinsky: *The Firebird*, "Finale" 163
Traditional American: *Joe Turner Blues* 160
Traditional American: *Johnny Has Gone for a Soldier* 184
Traditional American: *When the Saints Go Marching In* 197
Traditional Mexican: *Cielito lindo* 194
Turner, et al: *Soulville* 14
Villa-Lobos: *The Little Train of the Caipira* 129
Wagner: *Die Walküre*, "Winterstürme" 139

POEMS AND LYRICS

Noise 136
River 147

THEME MUSICAL

Don't Go Anywhere Without a Song 210
Everything's Coming Up Roses 214
I Like Me 213
Never Say Never 215

Song Index

12 All for the Best   254
12 America   257
9 America, the Beautiful   166
12 As Long As He Needs Me *(Oliver!)*   234

10 Beating the Blahs   190
9 By the Waters of Babylon   171

5 California, Here I Come   111
2 Chester   34
8 Con el vito   154
10 Coney Island Baby   188
12 Consider Yourself *(Oliver!)*   225

8 Dancin'   150
6 De colores   130
4 Dedication   83
10 Dodi Li   175
12 Dona nobis pacem   257
11 Don't Go Anywhere Without a Song   210

1 Elegua   13
12 Erie Canal   258
11 Everything's Coming Up Roses   214

4 Fiddler, The   85
11 Food, Glorious Food *(Oliver!)*   217
6 Fugue in G   134

12 Gaudeamus omnes in Domino   259
11 Gilu Hagalilim   200, 201, 202
11 Glee Reigns in Galilee   200, 201, 202

5 Hatikvah   104
5 Hello, My Baby   100
12 He's Got the Whole World in His
      Hands   263
12 Here We Come A-Singing   260
6 Home on the Rolling Sea, A   133
12 Hosanna   264
3 How Troubled the Waters   53
4 Hunter, The   78

12 I Like It Here   265
11 I Like Me   213
12 I Love Pasta   266
13 I Love the Mountains   269
1 I Ride an Old Paint (medley)   30
12 I'd Do Anything *(Oliver!)*   230
5 I'd Like to Teach the World to Sing   107
13 If   270
9 If I Were You   171
6 I'm an Old Cowhand   126
2 In the Army   44
9 It's Not So Easy Bein' Me   160

1 Ja Da   6
13 Jolly Old St. Nicholas   271
5 Just in Time   110

4 King of Love My Shepherd Is, The   79
4 Kyrie   74

10 Laredo   186
11 Let It Snow   204

13 Mangwani Mpulele   272
9 Manipulations   168
4 Marine's Hymn, The   99, 173
13 Mary Ann   275
4 Men of Harlech   95
13 Mermaid, The   275
5 Merry Minstrels   103
2 Metronome, The   50
5 Mi caballo blanco   118
13 Mighty Fortress Is Our God, A   276
5 My White Horse   118

11 Never Say Never   215
1 Nine Hundred Miles   7
13 Noble Dame   278
2 NonChester   35

6 Ode to Joy   135
1 Oh Dear, What Can the Matter Be?   11
8 Oh, Susanna *(arrangement in 7)*   151
4 Old Abram Brown   99
4 Old Hundred   72
9 On My Journey   170
4 One of Those Songs   97
13 One Tin Soldier   279

13 Puttin' On the Style   280

13 Raisins and Almonds   281
2 Red River Valley (medley)   30
12 Reviewing the Situation *(Oliver!)*   240
8 River *(lyrics only)*   147
9 Rock Around the Clock   158
5 Rose, The   117
5 Row, Row, Row Your Boat   113
13 Rozhinkes mit Mandlen   281

13 Sakura   282
8 Scatterbox   142
13 Scattin' with Solfège   285
4 See Sharp   57
13 Sentimental Journey   289
1 Sing   5
13 So My Sheep May Safely Graze   290
2 Songs of the West (medley)   30
13 Spring Song   291
14 Star-Spangled Banner, The   292
14 Step to the Rear   293
2 Streets of Laredo (medley)   30

6 Tell Me Why   132
14 Thanksgiving Calypso   298
5 This Land Is Your Land   114
8 This Old Hammer   148
9 Those Magic Changes   161
14 Time in a Bottle   300

Reference Bank   317

14 Tina Singu   301
14 Try to Remember   301
5 Tumbalalaika   120

4 Water Come a Me Eye   84
4 We're All Together Again   80
10 When the Saints Go Marching In   196
2 Where Have All the Flowers Gone?   28
11 Where Is Love? *(Oliver!)*   222

4 While Strolling Through the Park One
  Day   81
12 Who Will Buy? *(Oliver!)*   236
14 Wi Yo He Yo   303

2 You Are My Sunshine   21
5 You're Never Fully Dressed Without a
  Smile   109
14 You've Got a Friend   304

Picture Credits

Contributing Artists: Katherine Ace; James Keith Birdsong; Glenna Hartwell; David McCall Johnston; Walt Sturrock; Andrea Vuocolo, David Wisniewski; Lane Yerkes.

Photographs: 2–3 Backgrounds: E.R. Degginger. 2: t. Sydney Byrd/Photo Trends; m. The Bettmann Archive; b. Ron Wolfson/LGI. 3: t. M. Nelson/FPG; m. Silver Burdett & Ginn; b. Stuart Cohen/Stock, Boston. 4: t. Silver Burdett & Ginn, courtesy of Temple Beth Ahm, Springfield, New Jersey; b.l. Nick Elgan/LGI; b.r. Victoria Beller-Smith. 9: Peter Arnold, Inc. 12: Hoa-Qui/Shostal Associates. 14: t.l. Sydney Byrd; t.r. Bob Frerck/Odyssey Productions; b. Ken Regan/Camera 5. 16: Mitchell Seidel. 17: The Bettmann Archive. 19: Silver Burdett & Ginn. 20: t. Bob Llewellyn/Four by Five, Inc.; b. Jack Tulling/Shostal Associates. 22: Courtesy, The New Music Consort. 24: Ed Blair/Shostal Associates; b. ESTO Photographs, Inc. 26: Victoria Beller-Smith for Silver Burdett & Ginn. 27: l. Silver Burdett & Ginn; r. Culver Pictures. 39: Jacques-Louis David, French, 1748–1825. *The Oath of the Horatii,* 1786, oil on canvas, 51¼ × 65⅝ in. (130.2 × 166.2 cm.) The Toledo Museum of Art, Toledo, Ohio. Gift of Edward Drummond Libbey. 42, 43: Silver Burdett & Ginn. 46: The Bettmann Archive. 47: t. Silver Burdett & Ginn; m. Steve Hamsen/Stock, Boston; b.l. Mark Solomon/LGI; b.r. Joe Viesti. 48, 49: Culver Pictures. 54: l. Culver Pictures; r. Mackson/FPG. 55: t. The Granger collection; b. Courtesy, U.S. Postal Service. 56: UPI/Bettmann Newsphotos. 62, 70, 84: Silver Burdett & Ginn. 92–93 Background: Wilson Goodrich/Tom Stack & Associates. 92: t. Steven Caras; m. Silver Burdett & Ginn; b. E. Nagele/FPG. 93: t. H. Armstrong Roberts; b. Silver Burdett & Ginn. 94: R. Thompson/Bruce Coleman. 98: Tom Meyers. 101: Silver Burdett & Ginn. 102: t.l. Ralph B. Pleasant/FPG: t.r. Patrice Ceisel/Stock, Boston; b. Silver Burdett & Ginn. 108: l. Alan Carey/The Image Works; m. Ann Hagen Griffiths/OPC; r. Silver Burdett & Ginn. 112: Silver Burdett & Ginn. 114: Clyde H. Smith/F-stop. 119: Robert Pastner/Shostal Associates. 122: Harry E. Parker/Bruce Coleman. 123: Carl Roessler/Click. Chicago, 124: Walter Chandoha. 128: Tom Rosenthal/Four by Five, Inc.; t.r. D. Ginssoui/FPG; b.l. Dan DeWilde for Silver Burdett & Ginn; b.r. Lenore Weber/OPC. 129: Silver Burdett & Ginn. 136: © Gerry Cranham/Photo Researchers, Inc. 138: l. Vera Roberts-Fotos International/Pictorial Parade; t.m. Martha Swope; b.m. Philippe Halsman/Magnum; t.r. Ferdinando Scianna/Magnum; b.r. Angie Coqueran/LGI. 139: l. James Heffernan/The Metropolitan Opera; r. Brink/Action Press. 142: D.G. MacLean/Shostal Associates. 144: Mitchell B. Reibel/Sports Chrome. 148: Silver Burdett & Ginn. 152: Syndication Ltd/Photo Trends. 153: Fetcher/Four by Five, Inc. 156: Dan DeWilde for Silver Burdett & Ginn. 157, 158: Silver Burdett & Ginn. 163: © 1985 Martha Swope. 164, 165: Silver Burdett & Ginn. 167: Purchase, with funds from the Burroughs Wellcome Purchase Fund; Leo Castelli; the Wilfred P. and Rose J. Cohen Purchase Fund; the Julia B. Engel Purchase Fund; the Equitable Life Assurance Society of the United States Purchase Fund; the Sondra and Charles Gilman, Jr. Foundation, Inc.; S. Sidney Kahn; the Lauder Foundation, Leonard and Evelyn Lauder Fund; the Sara Roby Foundation; and the Painting and Sculpture Committee Acq. #84.6. Photo by Geoffrey Clemens. 172: J. Messerschmidt/Bruce Coleman. 182–183 Background: Kevin Schafer/Tom Stack & Associates. 182: t.l. J. Allan Cash LTD/Shostal Associates; t.r. © 1986 Ted Rice/Exposed Images; b. Reagan Bradshaw. 183: t. Culver Pictures; b. Shostal Associates. 184: Ron Sherman/Bruce Coleman. 185: Anne Rippey. 187: The Bettmann Archive. 192: Shostal Associates. 193: Allan A. Philiba. 194: Margaret C. Berg/Berg & Associates. 195: Gabler/FPG. 197: Robert Frerck/Odyssey Productions. 208, 209: Silver Burdett & Ginn. 252–253 Background: Rod Planck/Tom Stack & Associates. 252: t. Joe Viesti; m. & b. Silver Burdett & Ginn. 253: t. © George Jones/Photo Researchers, Inc.; b.l. Robert Frerck/Odyssey Productions; b.r. Eric Carle/Bruce Coleman.

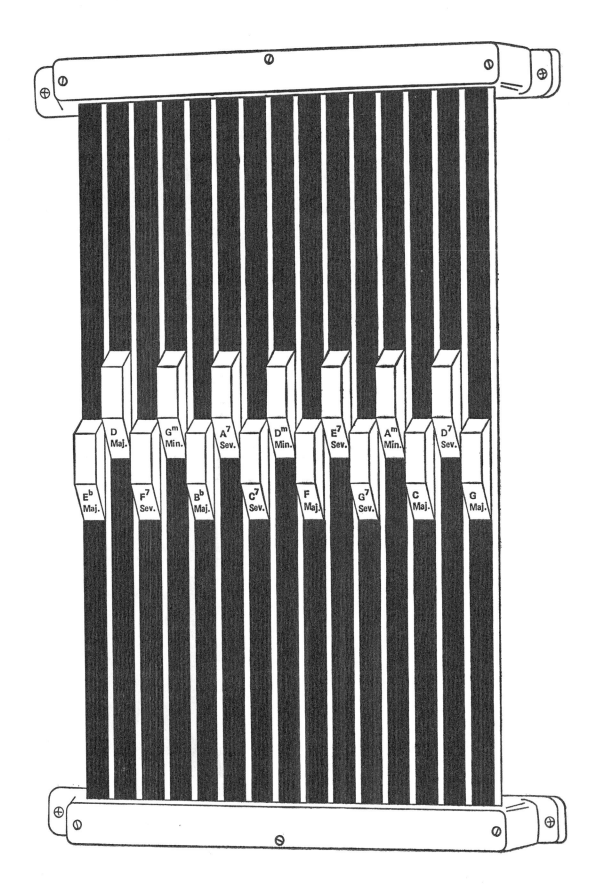